D1587404

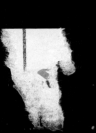

Sparkman & Stephens

Classic Modern Yachts

Sparkman & Stephens

Classic Modern Yachts

Franco Pace

Text by John Lammerts van Bueren

Foreword by Olin J. Stephens II

WoodenBoat Books
Brooklin, Maine, USA

Adlard Coles Nautical
London

Acknowledgements

We are honoured and ever grateful for the tireless support of Olin J. Stephens II.

Published 2002 by Adlard Coles Nautical
an imprint of A & C Black Publishers Ltd
37 Soho Square, London W1D 3QZ
www.adlardcoles.co.uk

Published 2002 in the USA by WoodenBoat Books
PO Box 78, Naskeag Road, Brooklin,
Maine, 04616 USA 1-800-273-SHIP(7447)
www.woodenboat.com

Copyright © Franco Pace 2002

ISBN 0-7136-6413-4 (UK)
ISBN 0-937822-75-2 (USA)

A CIP catalogue record for this book is available from the British Library.

Note: While all reasonable care has been taken in the publication of this book, the publisher takes no responsibility for the use of the methods or products described in the book.

Typeset in 11pt on 14pt Galliard
Printed and bound in Italy

Contents

The Design Process

by Olin J. Stephens II

The design of a yacht can be and has been done in many different ways and with much or little sophistication. This has been exemplified in my own work when you realize how untutored, in any scientific or technical sense, I was in the beginning. With application and experience I was able to learn 'on the job'. I was lucky to have friends who were teachers, especially Ken Davidson, in the early days of model testing. That is not to say that I ever mastered the kind of mathematics that I would need to understand all of today's methods, or, conversely, that there are not even now some good boats being designed and built with the use of very little beyond intuition and a good eye for line. Common sense and balance, in an overall sense, are useful guides. One might not think first of design as a form of communication but understanding the owner's wishes is a key to their proper interpretation. The owner must convey and the designer must grasp a set of wishes and purposes. That done, the designer must communicate to the builder the information that will result in the embodiment of the owner's expectations. Recently I have seen great changes in the way designers communicate with builders. There are many variables for the owner and designer to arrange in a hierarchy of importance as moderated by practical considerations. Different purposes have their needs. Racing has its class subdivisions ranging widely over size and venue, but within a class the needs are well defined and speed is a clear target. Cruisers and cruiser-racers require more compromise. The designer, however unsophisticated, has inherited through the boats he knows the experience of history, from the floating log through the dugout canoe to the big carbon-fibre dinghies of today. Technology and scale have changed and some of the waypoints suggest how and why.

Probably the first step was practical: adding planks to the dugout or more logs to the raft; propulsion evolved too, oars and sails were being used. Leading areas were the Nile of Egypt and the Mediterranean of Greece followed by Italy. The first scientist was Archimedes who related buoyancy to volume. Ships had grown by this time as shown by remains found by divers. China's technology for some time grew separately and the chinese seem to have been first with very large vessels and compass navigation, though the Greeks had understood latitude since Homer's time. The Scandinavian warriors and the traders of northern Europe took to the sea around the Twelfth Century. Science, marked by Euclid and the compass, reached Europe through Venice around 1400. In 1565 a Portuguese priest and sailor, Oliveira, wrote possibly the first general book on shipbuilding. The Sixteenth Century saw the mass production, using sub-assemblies, of ships and galleys in the Venice *Arsenale*.

A long step in science was made by Newton who introduced measurable dynamics in 1695. The hydrodynamic implications of his work were interpreted in Basle by the Bernoullis and Euler, both theoretical and practical, and were applied to ship design, construction and handling in the classic work, *Traite de Navire*, by the French astronomer, Pierre Bouguer, in 1745. Such work led to model tests proposed, perhaps done, by Benjamin Franklin to predict performance, as reported by Chapman in 1768. However, it was not until 1875 that William Froude in England successfully related ship and model drag, and naval architecture entered the modern era. Froude's insight was to realize that ship resistance could be split into parts and that each part required different treatment to correctly relate model and ship scale. Friction, drag, and wave making are the most important elements of resistance. Supported by confidence in Froude's analysis, science and technology began exponential gains, benefiting commerce and the growing industrial world. Science, supported by industry in the Nineteenth Century, brought steam propulsion. Paddle wheels, used first, inefficient when heeled at sea and easily damaged in conflict, were replaced by screw propellers. Clippers and packet ships marked top commercial sail performance. Leading designers in America were Donald McKay and Will H. Webb. Supported by technology and steam power, iron and steel replaced wood in examples like the *Great Eastern* and the Civil War ironclads. Yacht racing used fore and aft sails, and the yacht *America*, in 1851, turned yachts around. Indeed, wide application of science and technology to yacht design followed successful small model testing, beginning in the mid 1930s. Model tests combined with sail coefficients provided the numbers for technical studies. Following the war came the adoption of the separated keel, rudder, and trim tab. GRP encouraged standardization, and Rule studies culminating in the Pratt project brought computers and the Velocity Prediction Programme (VPP) fully into design, bringing new awareness of effects of individual parameters. As the century ended, accumulated understanding applied to new materials for hulls and sails offered new speed possibilities.

'Yachts' were first seen in Holland and came to England with Charles II when he returned to the throne in 1682. The people of Holland had presented him with a small ship. Racing using time allowances began around 1800 with races among the yachts of the Royal Yacht Squadron. Larger boats were recognised as faster than the smaller ones, and a Squadron member named

PREVIOUS DOUBLE PAGE: *The mighty J-Class* Ranger *charging along.* Ranger *was a joint effort between Starling Burgess and Olin Stephens. Her performance was superior to any J-Class sloop ever built.* OPPOSITE: Ranger, *seen off Newport, Rhode Island after finishing her fourth and final race, securing the 1937 America's Cup with a clean sweep.*

Acker estimated the time for each ton of cargo that a larger yacht should allow to a smaller one on the cross-Channel course. Later, for other courses, the distance was divided by the time, to establish time-per-mile for any course length. British nobles followed the king as yacht owners, and Froude's yacht design evolved as a speciality. As racing developed the fleet grew. At first they showed their ability by carrying out naval manoeuvres; soon racing followed. The early yachts were small naval vessels but fishing types were used more and more. With the demand for speed, the importance of rating rules became evident and new regulations were analysed. British tonnage measurements penalised beam; American rules penalised freeboard. Better understanding of the parameters length, sail area, and displacement brought new rules and better boats. The International Rule in Europe and Universal Rule in America, RORC and CCA for offshore, IOR and IMS, were all established to become a complex system of rules leading to the growth of one-design classes.

I see such history as the scaffolding that supports the modern yacht designer as he proceeds with his work. The start requires a generalised picture of the boat to come. The test of practicability comes from the materialisation of the requirements as a freehand sketch of an arrangement plan. Berth lengths of two metres offer

OPPOSITE: *A launching at Minneford, City Island, New York.*
ABOVE: *The yawl* Odyssey *is launched in 1935 at the Nevins Yard, City Island, New York.*
RIGHT: *Cheers! Olin and Rod Stephens are on board with their client and good friend Eddie Grief.*

a scale. We can take this sketch as the first stage of a spiral that begins with a highly provisional assessment of the possibilities in order to test ideas and coordinate tentative dimensions. Its purpose and use vary according to the owner's requirements and the means to meet them.

First choices are more or less firm according to the designer's experience in meeting those requirements. Choosing the fundamental parameters length, displacement and probably beam, it is possible to assume further values that are implied – importantly, wetted area and its concomitant, sail area. The selection of these values is tentative because of the degree in which they are interdependent; sequence is important and the interdependency must end in full consistency. Weights, consistent with the assumed dimensions, are usually studied first as a key to the other values. Displacement must be great enough to provide for a strong hull and rig, including ballast to give stability sufficient to support the desired sail area as a multiple of wetted area. The ratio of sail area to wetted area is a valuable index of light-weather performance.

The approximation of hull and rig weight can be based on rules of thumb, often expressed in a simple computer programme – in the Sixties the hand calculator replaced the slide rule. Materials and conditions of purpose and use result from the structural requirements. A scantling rule is a useful guide but most such rules are dependent on displacement, meaning that some guesswork is still needed to enter the spiral. Experience helps to tighten the spiral. We can be confident that the greater the sail in relation to wetted area, the better will be the

performance in light airs, yet to support the rig in stronger winds, good stability is needed. There is clear opposition between wetted area and stability as a zero-sum game and a choice, balanced to suit expected weather, is the only answer. The relation between wetted area and lateral plane comes into play largely as a function of the aspect ratio of the keel. With the high-aspect ratio associated with deep-draft keel area, wetted area can be reduced, but rule requirements or the owner's wishes usually set maximum draft, thus limiting aspect ratio.

When the design has reached the point where tentative values have been found for the principal dimensions, the next firm step will be to evaluate the righting moment as derived through metacentric height. Here let me recall Bouguer who derived the concept and calculation in 1745. Today it is a key to performance. The righting moment is the product of the displacement and the transverse separation of the centres of buoyancy and gravity as a boat heels. That is a function of metacentric height which can be found from the hull dimensions, generally increasing with beam. It is readily calculated or presented by computer software but is still dependent on the relative location of the centres of buoyancy and gravity, functions of hull geometry and structure. Accurate location of the centre of gravity is not difficult but is laborious. It, too, is initially estimated as various elements of the spiral are firmed up by repetition; it can be compared with the centre of buoyancy. A friend, Fred Dellenbaugh, suggested a simple coefficient to relate metacentric height to sail area.

I think of the primary values as length (L), displacement (D), sail area (S), beam and draft. When these dimensions describe a workable boat the lines are drawn. A VPP is useful to check performance and to evaluate possible changes. In the absence of computers, lines are done by hand on a prepared net or sheet on which are first drawn the lines that locate the several planes that turn one dimension into three. Conventionally the views consist of profile with buttock lines, waterlines, diagonals, and body plan or sections. These can be visualized by looking at a loaf of sliced bread. The profile is the side view, and the sections are the slices. Not so evident are the waterlines and diagonals, but the former are like contours of horizontal slices and the diagonals are similar but at chosen angles between horizontal and vertical. Nor can we see on the loaf the buttock lines, which are the surface intersections of vertical planes parallel with the centreline.

As done by hand, the longer longitudinal lines were 'faired', that is drawn with flexible splines or battens, usually wood, held to predetermined points with so-called ducks, which are lead weights with extended bills or points to hold the splines. Points that have been located by coordinates in one view must be exactly duplicated in all views. The actual drafting can be quick or extended, depending on experience, and similarly it can be accurate or sloppy. It has now been completely displaced by computers.

LEFT: *Two men studying a keel model from the J-Class* Rainbow.
OPPOSITE: *The men at Bath Ironworks have just started laying the deck on J-Class* Ranger. *Note the diagonal straps stiffening the hull.*
FOLLOWING DOUBLE PAGE: Ranger *under construction at Bath Ironworks. Commissioned by Mr. Harold Vanderbilt, this J-Class would go down in history as the fastest sloop ever built.*

Predetermined points may be located either by eye or by formula. Maximum beam would normally be set as the result of stability calculations, and shape of the datum waterline (DWL) toward either end would usually be a tabulated function of the maximum at some station into which the length had been divided. The mid section could be drawn by eye or with some preferred curve. The area was controlled by values chosen for displacement and prismatic coefficient. I considered area, denoted as the prismatic coefficient, extremely important. I used a diagonal through the centreline at the DWL with its high point at the mid-section and station offsets as useful control points. With this diagonal, the waterline, and the profile or canoe-body contour, the fairing process could continue with the

hull shape pretty well set. I once did the lines of a successful boat in one long working day, say eleven hours, but that was anticipating the visit of a client and was quick. A computer would cut that time way down. Until the Sixties all of the numerical work except ratings was done with a slide rule. Ratings were done with logarithms. Now the computer does it all, but the principles and the human decisions remain the same.

Before computers, lines were sent to the builders as a table of offsets that gave the dimensions from a centreline or base line to the hull surface. The net used for the lines drawing was enlarged to full scale on the builder's mould loft floor. Using those dimensions the original was essentially duplicated, though the difficulty of perfectly locating some points made it

supplemented by accommodation plan and deck plan, to which may be added few or many details dependent on the size of the boat and the requirements of the builder.

The plans of the yacht depend on more than the process I have described. That is always the product of the architect's ideas and values. I made such efforts as I could to uphold the values that made S&S-designed yachts what they were as practical and useful hardware. There were standards built into the plans and there was follow-up at the yards. Strength was a top priority, as was the principle that below decks must be kept dry. Decks and rigs should be laid out for ease of handling whether for racing or cruising. Blocks took lines to winches at the right height and angle and then to cleats where the angle was right again. The steering gear had to be free and easy, under one pound per foot. Rod measured that. Such details were part of the design. Good appearance was equally required.

I had always in mind the matter of balance, not only on the helm, but in all design elements. I thought of balance – end for end, above water vs. below, sail area vs. lateral plain and as broadly as possible in the whole design – as the avoidance of

PREVIOUS DOUBLE PAGE: *Launching day for* Ranger. *The yard crew rallies, teaming up all together to drive wedges transferring the weight of the boat on to the greased ways.*

LEFT: Ranger *charges down the runway.*

BELOW: *Olin Stephens at the wheel of* Ranger, *with Mrs. Gertrude Vanderbilt standing behind him. As part of the regular afterguard she would often join the crew, constantly observing the competition.*

customary to check their location at full size using longer and stiffer battens.

Usually the designer would make a point of watching such fairing and, in a highly visible line such as the sheer, might make a change. With computer lines drawn with good software the lines can be considered perfectly correlated at all points, and patterns can be cut by computer without going through the lofting stage.

I stress the lines drawing but, obviously, there is more to do. A sail plan is needed and offers a good chance to study the boat's appearance – importantly the sheer and freeboard, and the balance of the ends. Structural materials and their arrangement are shown on the inboard profile and section. These are

extremes. That last might be excepted in racing boats. There, with the uncertainty of much yacht design, I made choices based on estimated probability. No matter how small the detail, if one choice seemed likely to be more favoured than its alternative, it was worth doing.

My active participation in design ended in 1980. I had formally retired on my 70th birthday in 1978. The problems of increasing age had caused the departure of other members of our strong team. I remained a very active consultant for another two years. Quitting regular attendance and commuting was a relief. I saw computers taking the place of drafting boards as symbols of the existence of change. It was time to let the new brooms sweep. Now, in 2002, all the individual boards have

gone, all except one or two used to spread out, for display or study, drawings that have been made by drafting machines directed by the computers.

Changed also is the subject and nature of the work. The number of projects has lessened while the size of each has correspondingly grown. I knew good years with 20 or more projects, most from 40 to 60 feet (12 to 18 metres) overall. Today many of the smaller boats are 'in house' designs, but an even wider horizon of yacht design is still putting food on the designer's table and it is rewarding to see how the work goes on.

Sparkman & Stephens continues to thrive. It is pleasant, without responsibility, to see that happening. The interest and the activity go on and the love of the subject, the design of good

yachts, is the same whether applied by computer or pencil and paper, slide rule and log tables or hand-held calculators; the power and flexibility they offer to a dedicated team is amazing.

Recently I have been pleased to recognise the classic shape of a new standardised 46-footer designed by S&S for the Walsted Shipyard in Denmark and I believe that their enthusiasm for her smaller size signals the breadth of their vision.

Factually, the proportion of larger yachts and powerboats is greater than it was and it seems likely to grow. Use of computers to handle graphics as well as calculations is a well recognized asset. All this is the nature of the modern design process.

Standing outside the circle my education continues. I am happy to follow the way the office is now going. My involve-

ment has been minimal, although I am occasionally asked for an opinion on hull shape or aesthetics. Personal interest in rating rules and in many aspects of the older boats, as well as yacht-design history, has caused me to lean on the office for many helpful answers. I have been invited to board meetings and enjoy the company of a new group and their way of facing a constantly changing world.

ABOVE: *Sheets eased*, Ranger *confidently powers along.*

Dorade

Year of build	1929
S&S Design number	7
Builder	Minneford Yacht Yard, City Island, New York
First owner	Roderick Stephens Sr.
Length overall	15.85 m
Length waterline	11.35 m
Beam	3.12 m
Draft	2.34 m
Displacement	17,150 kg

Newport, Rhode Island, USA, July 4th 1931, a small white sailing boat impatiently tugs at her mooring lines, longing to go to sea. It's *Dorade* and she's almost the smallest of a fleet of yachts entering the Transatlantic Race to Plymouth on the south coast of England. Her lines are very different from those of the other competitors. She measures just under 16 m in length and looks very tender with her narrow beam. Her rigging appears much lighter than the eye is used to. Her crew, averaging 22 years of age and made up of a group of friends and Olin's younger brother Rod, are considered too young for such a demanding race across the Atlantic. *Dorade*'s skipper Olin Stephens, a man of just 23, also happens to be the yacht's designer. (None of the crew has ever sailed the Atlantic before.) Some observers even feel the Club should not allow such fragile boats as *Dorade* to take part.

Roderick Stephens Sr., father of the young Stephens brothers, joined the crew. Two years earlier, he had sold the family business and decided to make a calculated bet on his sons' abilities by commissioning *Dorade*. Sparkman & Stephens was a young company and could do with the publicity of a winning

TOP LEFT: Dorade*'s tiller, simple and elegant.*
BELOW: *The foredeck: the hatches have survived the test of time.*
OPPOSITE: Dorade *during her first race at the 1997 Veteran Boat Rally off the coast of Sardinia.*
FOLLOWING DOUBLE PAGE: *Porto Cervo 1997.* Dorade *immediately won the first event after her restoration.*

design. His confidence was rewarded in the first season when she finished second in class in the Bermuda Race. Although *Dorade* did not attract much attention at that time, she held great promise for her crew. They also learned from the Bermuda Race that she was slightly over-canvassed and consequently the small bowsprit was removed, resulting in a beautifully balanced yawl.

At last her crew felt it was time for the big race across the Atlantic. After careful consideration they opted for the Great Circle Route, which is more or less the route that planes take today when flying from London to New York. Although this course was the shortest, it did not offer them the advantage of favourable currents in the Gulf Stream and it would take them to an area notorious for fog and icebergs. After studying the magazines and literature the consensus was that the shorter distance would still outweigh the advantages of the favourable current and so *Dorade* set her course north, with almost the entire fleet taking the southerly route.

Dorade was sailed well and raced hard as were the other boats in the fleet. With her new hand-sewn mainsail, bought for the race by the grandparents of the Stephens brothers, she averaged 200 miles and more on many days, quite remarkable for a boat of her size. Although her narrow beam made her roll heavily downwind, those same fine lines made her slice through the waves; she proved herself a great sea boat.

It was 'Land Ho!' on the 16th day at Bishop's Rock and the next morning *Dorade* sailed closely past the lighthouse at Lizard Point to exchange signals. The signalman at Lizard Point hoisted code flags E over C meaning: 'What ship is this?' Quickly the crew of *Dorade* responded by hoisting code flag H, meaning '*Dorade*'. After a short interval the flag was lowered and on *Dorade* the code flags CTV were hoisted, 'Which am I?' Without hesitation the signalman replied NAX, 'YOU ARE FIRST'. The lighthouse keeper continued to observe the little white yawl, waiting for her crew to acknowledge his signal when he saw complete pandemonium break out on board: men were slapping each other on the shoulder, dancing and leaping up and down the deck. At the tiller stood a young man wearing spectacles and a wide grin. Today Olin recalls that moment as one of the happiest of his life; it was certainly one of the most significant moments for the office of Sparkman & Stephens as that first offshore victory added their name to the list of well-known successful naval architects.

As *Dorade* continued her course to Plymouth, the race committee sent out a launch to greet the winner. But the launch motored past *Dorade* without recognising her. The skipper simply could not believe that such a clean and tidy boat had just crossed the Atlantic. He continued his search for some battered craft while *Dorade* made her way to port. Out at sea, two large

TOP LEFT: Dorade *gave her name to a vent that would serve on almost every ocean-going yacht.*
BELOW: *The old fittings from the thirties never left the boat.*
OPPOSITE: Dorade *slicing through the water in a gentle breeze off Santo Stefano.*
FOLLOWING DOUBLE PAGE: Dorade *sailing close-hauled near Santo Stefano.*

ocean racers, *Highland Light* and *Landfall*, were battling within each other's sight. Racing so close after crossing the Atlantic, their skippers undoubtedly imagined they were leading the fleet home. *Dorade* decided to greet them the next morning and so headed back to sea. As *Landfall* approached Plymouth a crewmember spotted the white yawl sailing towards them. 'Looks like *Dorade*,' he said. 'Don't even joke about that,' replied skipper Paul Hammond, but as the yacht came closer they realised that *Dorade* had indeed beaten them to the line by two days, without even calling on handicap. On corrected time *Dorade* had a winning margin of four days but as every sailor knows, having line honours made the victory even sweeter.

Dorade went on to win England's most famous offshore event, the Fastnet Race. The critics were proved wrong again and the yachting press wrote in awe of the fine qualities of *Dorade* and her well-thought-out design and deck layout. Everything was right, where a cleat or fitting was needed there was one, and every fitting was placed at the correct angle. Her young crew handled her beautifully and she was quick beyond belief, out-sailing most of the fleet under almost any conditions. Demonstrating some great seamanship, Rod Stephens was seen one day sailing the engineless *Dorade* into port single-handed, picking up his mooring, stowing the sails and jumping on board *Arrow*, an International 14, in less than eight minutes. To add to the story, Rod won the 14's race too!

Dorade was hoisted on board a steam-liner and joined by her crew to make her way back to New York. Lightening the days of the Great Depression, the Mayor of New York granted the victorious crew a ticker-tape parade on Broadway, the first ever for a winning crew of an offshore yacht race. Without doubt the concept and performance of *Dorade* revolutionised offshore-racing design. Although a change of rules would soon penalise her narrow beam, the general concept would remain an example for offshore racing boats in decades to come.

In 1996 Dr. Giuseppe Gazzoni Frascara purchased *Dorade* and shipped her to the Cantiere Navale dell'Argentario where *Dorade* would undergo her restoration. The yard had already made their mark with the spectacular restoration of the S&S 12-Metre, *Nyala*, and would soon prove that *Dorade* was in good hands. The yard's manager, Federico Nardi, fell head over heels for *Dorade* and dedicated a hand-picked crew of the finest craftsmen to the project. The work was done with no apparent budget restrictions and the result was an uncompromised project reviving *Dorade* to her former glory. Her deck was completely replaced as well as a good number of beams. Although some of the lower planks inevitably had to be replaced, most of her planking and frames proved sound. The small cabin top and hatches were in good shape but part of the cockpit had to be renewed.

Naturally the yard meticulously followed the original design. Many of her original fittings were still on board and would be re-used. The dorade vents, where visibly important, were rebuilt to the old design. (The vents were invented by Rod Stephens who, in search of improved ventilation at sea, came up with the idea to place a horn-shaped ventilator on a box. The outlet was then offset against the passage through the deck and the box would have a limber hole for any water to escape. The simplicity

of the idea confirmed Rod's genius in such things. With *Dorade* being the first to carry these vents, the 'dorade' vent was born. The vent and the name are still in use on yachts throughout the world to this day.) A major part of the restoration project was to return the interior to the original design. Few detailed drawings were available but, with help from the office of Sparkman & Stephens and Olin himself, she came as close to original as one could expect.

The invitation to the launching party was an opportunity for Olin to reacquaint himself with his first successful design. It was a happy reunion and the start of a new friendship between designer and yard. Happy to see *Dorade* the way she was at the start of his long career, Olin enjoyed sailing her in the beautiful waters of Tuscany in the company of good friends. He would often return and receive a hero's welcome in the small town of Porto Santo Stefano.

A new chapter was added to the life of that little white yawl as she entered the Mediterranean circuit of classic yacht regattas and it would not be complete without mentioning her new skipper and custodian, Giles McLaughlin. Giles took great pride in his care of *Dorade* and, wherever he sailed her, she would be clean and tidy with her bronze fittings shining.

As for the races in the Mediterranean, it seemed *Dorade* came full circle. From the outset she did extremely well. The first outing was at Porto Cervo, Sardinia. She won every single race on corrected time and with the last race she took line honours, even showing a clean transom to the large schooners such as *Mariette*. The crew was excited to see the old girl do so well but for *Dorade* it seemed no more than routine. There was really no reason to think she would do anything less than best: after all, she had won all the major ocean races of her time; now the Mediterranean circuit was to be hers too.

In 2000 *Dorade* was sold to Dutchman Peter Frech. He continues to race and cruise her around the coasts of Europe and keeps her in immaculate condition. A special place is reserved in the hearts of all those who have experienced the delight of sailing *Dorade*, the great little yawl that changed the face of ocean racing.

OPPOSITE: Dorade *on a close reach.*
FOLLOWING DOUBLE PAGE: *The main saloon, all in the finest mahogany. Her narrow beam makes life rather tight below.*

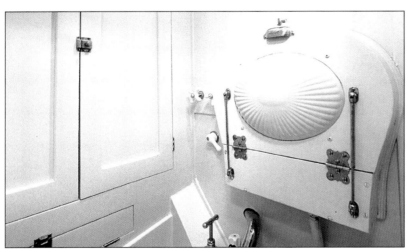

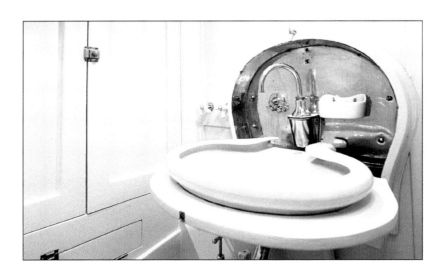

Dorade & Design

In 1929 a young man burned the midnight oil at his drawing board, drafting what was to become a milestone in offshore-racing yachts. He had worked on a couple of 6-Metre designs and understood the underlying hydrostatics and calculations that applied to these narrow, deep hulls. The previous year he had been part of the delivery crew sailing a 10-Metre from Halifax to New York. At sea, the shape of the Metre boats gave a swift and confident motion but he soon learned that long and full overhangs had to be avoided in offshore boats.

No doubt the Metre boats inspired Olin Stephens' design for *Dorade*. For any yacht designer it is remarkable to design a boat that so convincingly outperforms the established fleet; even more so if that design happens to be the first offshore design of a 21-year-old who has previously only designed a small number of boats such as dinghies and 6-Metres. *Dorade* was Olin's seventh design. Lacking formal education as a naval architect, Olin's guidelines were limited to reading and intuition. The rating rule at the time seemed to accommodate a large variety of designs and contemporary naval architects appeared fairly relaxed about it. Few, if any, tried to design offshore yachts to the limit. With *Dorade*, Olin Stephens found an opening.

The first ocean racer by Sparkman & Stephens differed from her contemporaries in many ways. Until then offshore yachts had ample beam and displacement; *Dorade* was narrow and light compared to the then-prevailing fisherman type offshore yachts. Her narrow beam compensated for her deep draft, and her easy sections seemingly moved her effortlessly through the waves with a relatively small sail area.

The typical yacht of that time had heavy grown-oak frames, but *Dorade* had narrow-spaced, steam-bent frames, saving weight and moving much of the rest down into the keel. Her masts were light, saving weight aloft; a reduction made possible by supporting the mast with three pairs of spreaders, holding it straight under every load. The combination of these factors made her a very quick boat that rated favourably. By no standards was she a design to the rule as we would see in today's world; only later would it become clear that small boats were much favoured by the rule.

The success of that first S&S offshore design was convincing, but in the process Olin became fascinated by rating rules, which would soon become the guidance for his work. He developed intimate knowledge of the rules in force on both sides of the Atlantic and soon mastered the art of combining numbers with intuition. Always seeking to develop in his work,

OPPOSITE TOP: *The galley, with a double sink.*
MIDDLE AND BELOW: *The beautiful Wilcox wash basin in the head folds up when not in use.*
LEFT: *The primary winches by Merryman. These were mounted in the early Fifties.*
ABOVE: Dorade *sailing close-hauled. Note her clean wake.*

Olin felt a strong desire to quantify the characteristics of his designs, only then could an objective comparison be made of the old and the new.

When, in the winter of 1932–33, Olin joined Professor Ken Davidson, working with him to define a correlation between scale models and full-size boats, his dreams for an opportunity to quantify the parameters that dominate the performance of his designs came true. Although research had a long way to go, the early results were promising. Even today, the learning curve has not come to an end. The tank will never design a yacht, but the comparative numbers deriving from each run help the naval architect to gain a deeper understanding of what makes or breaks a good design. Olin's fascination for the science behind

the art made him a valued member on the Rating Rule committees of the North American and the International Yacht Racing Unions and later the International Offshore Rule and Offshore Racing Council.

As his dreams for a reliable VPP continued, the complexity of calculations required computing abilities that could hardly be considered affordable in the Sixties. But a machine that could do the job happened to be just around the corner from Sparkman & Stephens, at the New York Stock Exchange. S&S were granted the opportunity to rent these mighty computers and so it came about that, after closing time at Wall Street, the S&S team would move office to make these machines run a very different set of numbers.

Clearly the scientific part of yacht design fascinated Olin Stephens on both a professional and personal level. The knowledge gained influenced his thinking and designs but never to the point that boats would become unsafe due to their proportions or construction. Throughout Olin's career, the same intuition that made *Dorade* a success would question the results of scientific experiments. Some designs shown in this book represented breakthroughs in yachting but, however radical some of the designs shown here may have been, they always retained a fine balance between speed, comfort, and beauty. The search for optimum rating and performance never led S&S to design boats that did not comply to what Olin and Rod Stephens had set as their minimum standards for safety at sea.

ABOVE: Dorade *sailing in Cannes, at the Régates Royales. In the background are* Velsheda *and* Moonbeam.

Restoring Stormy Weather

When Federico Nardi of the Cantiere Navale dell' Argentario first visited *Stormy Weather*, her life had been a very busy one. She was designed to race hard and that's just what she had done. Boats are driven to the limit during offshore races and *Stormy* was no exception. During her 65 years she didn't have much time to relax; probably no other boat had entered so many offshore races and she had made close to 30 Atlantic crossings. The fact that she held out so long is a credit to the yard of Nevins as well as to her owners who took care of her between races. The first large refit was done in the Eighties by Paul Adamthwaite who, guided by Rod Stephens, fitted new laminated frames and replaced a good number of planks, making her ready for a new life. Paul lived on board *Stormy* for some 20 years, passing his time racing, cruising, and chartering in the Caribbean until, in 1999, he sailed her to Lake Ontario and put her up for sale. Soon afterwards Federico Nardi bought her on behalf of a client and had her shipped to his yard in Tuscany. Unlike many contemporary restoration projects of today, *Stormy* was not rescued from the brink; she was still fit to sail, although Federico knew that she was tired and ready for a major overhaul.

Lucky enough to have found a client ready to foot the bill for a scrupulous restoration, the Cantiere was able to approach the project thoroughly, preparing the yacht for another generation to come. When a new restoration project comes to the yard the first job is to find her original drawings and building specifications as well as photographs of the yacht's early days. These will guide the craftsmen as they assess what needs to be

done to bring her back to the way she was. Finding these papers is usually a strenuous job but fortunately the office of Sparkman & Stephens had detailed drawings available and photos were found at the Rosenfeld collection in Mystic Seaport.

The next step is hauling the boat into the yard for a thorough inspection. Typically the suspect areas are the extreme far ends where there is limited ventilation. Suspect areas are scraped back to bare wood for further inspection. *Stormy*'s stem was found to be soft and had to be replaced. Bent frames tend to break in areas of narrow curves and greatest stress. Down in the bilge they often turn soft and, worse, if steel frames have been employed, corrosion often affects the structure of the wood, turning it black and brittle.

PREVIOUS DOUBLE PAGE: Stormy Weather *at the Cantiere Navale dell'Argentario. Her topsides are scraped back and she is almost ready for the first protective coat of paint.* OPPOSITE TOP: *Her topsides remain painted as long as possible to prevent the wood from drying out.* MIDDLE: *The soft planks are removed and replaced one by one.* BOTTOM LEFT: *Most frames on* Stormy *were in acceptable condition, but the planking under the waterline needed a lot of attention.* BOTTOM RIGHT: *The planks are tapered in both directions, the edges are bevelled, the shape of the hull requires the planks to be bent and twisted, and in the end all has to fit tight as a bottle. Here the planks join the horntimber; often a tricky corner.* THIS PAGE: *The planks are now almost in place and are fastened with Everdur bronze screws. Sunk below the surface of the planks, the bronze screws are hidden by a wooden plug giving a smooth hull. Its a labour intensive job, as each screw has a plug and each plug is cut off by hand and faired to the shape of the hull by sanding.*

This is where the merits of rebuilding American boats comes to light. Unlike most European yards, the men in the New World used bronze rather than steel for floors and frames. *Stormy* was built at Nevins and was one of those iron-free boats. This probably saved her backbone and wooden keel – an awesome chunk of solid oak measuring 74x15 cm. Oak is particularly prone to deterioration when in contact with steel. *Stormy* had eight bronze floors supporting the mast step and oak floors throughout the rest of the boat.

It soon became apparent that it was not the materials of the past that were in bad shape, but the ones used in the 'modern age'. Epoxy coatings had locked moisture into the timber, causing a gradual decay in the lower planks and frames, and all had to be replaced. The job of finding the right mahogany was assigned to Piero, the master shipwright.

The yard takes great pride in using the originally specified species of wood. Unfortunately, the Philippine mahogany is simply no longer available in the required length so Federico opted for a 9-metre-long log of select Grand Bassam mahogany. Grand Bassam was a mahogany often used for planking in the Thirties as it was (and is) available in long and clear lengths with diameters up to 1.8 m. To ensure the colour and structure of the wood was uniform, an entire log was purchased for *Stormy* and was cut to the specific sizes required. The next step was to dry the wood. In the old days this would be done naturally, by carefully stacking the wood and leaving it to dry for three years or more. Today the tremendous cost of the wood forces the yards to use artificial kiln drying. With sophisticated computer programmes the temperature in the kiln is gradually increased and the moisture driven out. To

bring the moisture content down to the required 15% takes about three weeks. The best yards will then leave the wood to relax for some months before the work on the planking starts.

A proper restoration is done from the bilge upwards and *Stormy Weather* was no different. It soon emerged that, apart from her sheer planks, her topsides were sound. Planks that could be saved remained painted during the restoration to prevent them from drying out. It was no surprise that nothing could be salvaged below the waterline. As the hull was dismantled, the new stem was constructed, after which planks were removed in pairs, ensuring the shape of the boat would be retained. Nevins's practice was to fasten the planks to the frames with Everdur-bronze screws rather than rivets and the yard followed that example. *Stormy Weather* had steam-bent frames of American white oak. Once the best-quality oak was selected, the frames were steam bent and fitted in position, bringing her back to the construction specification Mr. Nevins had in mind when he built her in the Thirties. The planking was fastened to the frames with screws driven through the 34 mm thick planking. Each screw was then protected from moisture by a

OPPOSITE TOP: *Preparing to lay the deck. The covering board is in place.* MIDDLE: *Splining the hull. The seams between the planking are carefully opened. A fine mahogany batten is fitted in the seam to stiffen the hull and help keep the topsides smooth.* BOTTOM: *The old winches are all disassembled and cleaned, after which they are hard chromed.* THIS PAGE: *The interior joinery is scraped back to the bare wood. The pride and joy of the craftsman is to perfectly match the old and the new by way of style, colour and construction. Many of the wood species used in the Thirties are very difficult to obtain today.*

wooden plug. The next step was to spline the hull. A flexible batten was used as a guide to cut a fine groove along the seams of the planking and a narrow mahogany spline was then fitted into the groove. Gluing the planks with splines distributes the loads on the hull, relieves the fastenings, and ensures stiff and smooth topsides, even under the warm Mediterranean sun. Once the planking was finished, the hull was faired using the hand planer and a sander. The craftsman was guided by his trained eye and hands; it is his job to finish the hull fair and smooth without filler.

Meanwhile the work on the deck commenced. *Stormy*'s original laid deck was long gone and had been replaced by teak over plywood. That had to come off so the deckbeams and beamshelf could be inspected. The beams were made of clear Sitka spruce, with the exception of the through beams at the mast, which were made of oak. Her shelf was Douglas-fir. Any suspect parts were replaced with the originally specified materials.

Her original aluminium-bronze chainplates had hardly suffered. They were fastened through the planking as well as the frames and through-bolted to the shelf. No wonder they had not moved since they left the yard in 1934. Before the new teak deck could be laid, a backplate for each deck fitting would be fitted to the beams to ensure the required strength for winches, tracks, and cleats. The deck hardware required a completely different skill. Where possible, old fittings were used or new ones were cast or fabricated following the 1934 designs of S&S, Nevins, and Merryman. Once all the fittings were complete they were chromed at the owner's request. Although most modern restorations have a teak deck on plywood, the yard opted for a traditionally laid deck, and not just

for the sake of originality. Teak-on-plywood decks have the serious drawback that, once they start to leak, the water is retained between the two layers resulting in early decay of the plywood. A properly laid teak deck is certainly watertight and if by any chance a leak does occur, it will be visible from the start and easily repaired.

Meanwhile the work on the interior started. The remaining original panelling was carefully scraped back to bare wood. For the missing parts mahogany was so carefully matched for texture and colour that even an expert could hardly distinguish the difference between the old and the new. Her cockpit had been altered several times and was reconstructed from scratch. Despite the efforts of the yard to rescue the original cabin-top the condition was such that it had to be built anew. It was made to fit the old deck structure like a hand in a glove. With dedication and fine craftsmanship the Cantiere Navale dell'Argentario gave *Stormy* another chance and secured her future for the next generation.

OPPOSITE TOP LEFT: *Lubricating the fastenings: a bronze screw is pulled through a piece of hard paraffin wax.* TOP RIGHT: *Laying the deck: the mahogany kingplank is carved to receive the teak strips.* MIDDLE: *Caulking the deck.* BOTTOM: *A circular saw bench is used to cut the strips to the right size.* THIS PAGE TOP RIGHT: *Bending the strips following the covering board. Clamps hold the strips in place while they are screwed down in the deck beams.* MIDDLE: *Bronze diagonal strips around the mast help distribute the loads of the rig.* BELOW LEFT: *A bandsaw is used to saw curves.* BELOW RIGHT: *Men will walk this ladder a thousand times.* NEXT DOUBLE PAGE: *Piero preserves the cabin top just before he carefully guides it into position.* FOLLOWING DOUBLE PAGE: *65 years old, and as new again.* Stormy Weather *is ready for re-launch.*

Stormy Weathe

Year of build	1934
S&S Design number	27
Builder	Henry Nevins,
	City Island, New York
First owner	Philip Le Boutillier
Length overall	16.43 m
Length waterline	12.12 m
Beam	3.81 m
Draft	2.39 m
Displacement	20,321 kg

Nㅤew York 1934; Philip Le Boutillier is enjoying dinner with his friends at 'The Manor' on Long Island, not long before the launch of his new S&S offshore-racing yawl at Nevins. They exchange ideas, talk boats and, in their minds, they are already on board, racing across the ocean on the new yawl. A young singer entertains the guests with a song by Harold Arlen. Liking the tune, Philip calls her over to the table and asks for an encore. 'Like it?' she asks, 'Like it?' Philip replied, 'You just named my new boat!' The young singer was Lena Horn, and the song 'Stormy Weather'.

Stormy Weather would become the most well known S&S offshore design of the Thirties. Her design followed in the wake of *Dorade*, the yawl that had put S&S on the map of winning designers just two years before. But the gap found by *Dorade* was no longer there; her narrow beam had been penalised by the revised rating rules; a new course in design had to be found. *Dorade* may have had her flaws but they were sufficiently hidden by her exceptional success. In the years between *Dorade* and *Stormy*, both Olin and his brother Rod had entered a steep learning curve.

Partner Drake Sparkman knew winning boats were priceless and, despite the dark days of the Great Depression, he was able to bring in new work to keep the office occupied. The orders were a nice balance between offshore and course racing, as well as some cruising yachts and motorboats. Some of the most successful designs in that period were the 6-Metres *Bob Cat* and *Cherokee*,

LEFT: *Dorade vents on* Stormy, *and her hardware shining like silver.*
OPPOSITE: Stormy Weather *making her way to windward in a fresh breeze off Santo Stefano.*
FOLLOWING DOUBLE PAGE: Stormy *at her best, smashing her way to windward. Olin Stephens is in the cockpit just behind the tiller; two old friends are united again.*

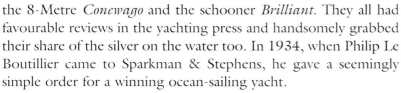

the 8-Metre *Conewago* and the schooner *Brilliant*. They all had favourable reviews in the yachting press and handsomely grabbed their share of the silver on the water too. In 1934, when Philip Le Boutillier came to Sparkman & Stephens, he gave a seemingly simple order for a winning ocean-sailing yacht.

No designer will ever be able to guarantee the success of his designs and for the young company of S&S their established reputation would remain on the line with each racing design that left the office. The new rules of the Cruising Club of America penalised narrow designs but, with what had been learned from *Dorade*, it is doubtful whether Olin would have opted for such a tender design again. Her extra beam would give *Stormy* the additional stability that made her a much better all-round boat. It would also give her a lot of extra space below; then again, for an offshore racing boat the accommodation comes by default as, on long passages, one needs to be able to sleep and cook. Although both Olin and Rod felt that some comfort could contribute to racing success, *Stormy*'s fine cruising abilities were probably a happy bonus rather than a priority design criterion. The weight of the interior was kept as minimal as possible by working with 6 mm mahogany panelling. This resulted in accommodation which, by contemporary standards, was rather spartan, but by today's it is comfortable beyond any doubt. She was built at Nevins on City Island under the watchful eye of Rod Stephens. Not that Mr. Nevins needed much guidance; his skills had a worldwide reputation. Rod's work would be to ensure the deck was laid to perfection: strong, simple and efficient, with fittings mounted where needed and cleats aligned with the fall of the winches.

With *Stormy Weather*, S&S delivered a design which met the dreams of her client; sailing fast under almost any conditions and rating favourably. Her lines were simple, clean and easily driven. After seeing her on the slipway at Nevins, the eminent yacht designer John Alden was quoted as saying, 'In my opinion a better design would be impossible to achieve.' And *Stormy* did well, winning the Transatlantic Race from Newport to Bergen, followed by the Fastnet Race, the Miami–Nassau Race, and the Bermuda Race. Rod Stephens skippered her on most occasions and was delighted with her seagoing abilities: a great all-round boat, at her best in strong winds.

Throughout his extended career with S&S, more than 2,000 designs carried Olin Stephens's signature. *Stormy Weather*'s attractive lines and seemingly endless string of victories made her rank among both Rod and Olin Stephens's favourite designs of the Thirties.

ABOVE LEFT TOP: *The ash tiller and mainsheet horse.* ABOVE LEFT: *This old South Coast winch never left* Stormy. ABOVE: *A full sail inventory.* OPPOSITE TOP: *The main saloon, all in fine mahogany. Compare her to* Dorade, *and the extra beam on* Stormy *certainly adds comfort and space below.* BOTTOM LEFT: *The galley in the forecastle with a gimballed cooker is simple and efficient.* BOTTOM RIGHT: *The self-bailing cockpit, with everything mounted in the right place.* NEXT DOUBLE PAGE: Stormy Weather *and* Latifa: *two contemporary ocean racers meet again off Santo Stefano.* FOLLOWING DOUBLE PAGE: *Back in her element,* Stormy Weather *is charging along at near hull speed during Argentario Week 2001.*

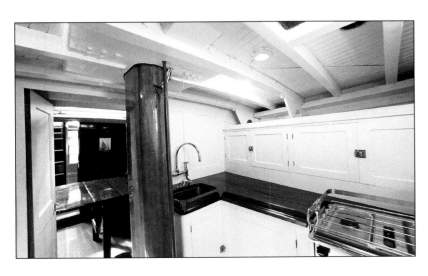

Metre Yachts

Seldom has a rating rule produced such a fleet of consistently beautiful thoroughbred racing yachts. For almost a century the Metre Rule has led naval architects to design the epitome of classic racing yachts with their sleek hulls, long overhangs, powerful rigs and deep keels. Probably no other class of boat gives such feeling of power, balance and speed when driven to windward. A gentle pull of the tiller reminds the helmsman that he needs to guide his boat back into the groove; once locked in, the yacht accelerates, making her crew feel at one with the wind and water.

At the beginning of the Twentieth Century yachts' racing scores were regularly determined by arbitrary handicap rules often designed to favour hosting clubs or countries. In 1907 the seafaring nations of Europe met in London to create a unified rating rule, which would allow individual designs to race without time allowance. They agreed upon what was to be known as the Metre Rule. Created as a full range of classes rating from 5- to 23-Metres, the 6-, 8- and 12-Metres soon emerged as the most popular. To date, their success is unprecedented as, 95 years on, Metre boat racing still attracts the world's best sailors and new yachts continue to be designed and built. Many Metre boats were created to win a single race or for a specific season, but thanks to the strict construction rules, they have lasted for generations.

Metre boats have been the choice for the world's most sought after short-course trophies. Olin Stephens was fascinated

by these yachts and, probably more than any other yacht designer of his time, he mastered the art of making them go fast. For almost 50 years all the major trophies in the Metre Classes have been won by his designs, most notably the America's Cup.

So what was it that differentiated these yachts from other classes? Knowing that a typical racing yacht has an active racing life of maybe five to ten years, how could these boats have survived for close to a century and remain competitive? The secret probably lies in the formula. Although it seems a simple playground to the mathematician, the infinite variables of the formula result in a range of hull shapes and sail plans that can keep any naval architect off the streets for a lifetime. In essence it is a length-versus-sail-area rule, meaning that the longer the boat, the less sail it can carry and vice versa, causing designers to suit the boat to the expected weather conditions: if the boat were designed to win a race in the Mediterranean then she would be short and light with a large sail area, and in windy locations such as the Clyde, Scotland, longer boats with less sail area would be favoured. The wind and weather, however, always remain factors the designer cannot control; it did not take long for them to learn that the most extreme designs seldom paid dividends.

Within the rule, differences of length, displacement and sail area, could vary as much as 20% from one boat to another. This seems sufficient to expect tremendous differences in performance but interestingly this was and is not the case. The framework in which the designs had to fit may have been flexible but the performance gains were marginal and the Lloyd's scantling rules also helped to keep performances fairly even.

Over the years the formula was amended three times but the weight and weight distribution rules have not been changed since 1908. Modern construction materials such as aluminium, GRP, and epoxies have their merits but, regardless of the fabrics used, the square weight of, for instance, the hull surface and deck had to remain the same, thus preventing the older wooden boats from instantly becoming obsolete. And last but not least, it takes a good sailor to make a good boat win; as proved by Olin Stephens himself, the best design does not necessarily guarantee a place on the podium.

THIS PAGE: *Freemantle 1986, the start of the International 12-Metre World Championships.*

Iroquois

Year of build	1967
S&S Design number	1862
Builder	Minneford, City Island, New York
First owner	Eugene van Voorhis
Length overall	14.03 m
Beam	2.46 m
Draft	2.05 m
Displacement	9,520 kg

When, in 1966, Eugene van Voorhis was looking for an Eight to regain The Canada's Cup for the Rochester Yacht Club he commissioned S&S to design *Iroquois*. Olin Stephens was also working on a Twelve named *Intrepid* to defend the America's Cup. *Iroquois* is regarded as an early offspring that benefitted much from *Intrepid*'s breakthrough design.

With the 1939 8-Metre, *Iskareen*, as a benchmark, five models were meticulously tested in the tank at the Stevens Institute of Technology until the final, perfect shape was found. That year *Iroquois* became the sensation of Lake Ontario. She was the first 8-Metre to sport a separated rudder and trim tab. Her mast was made in aluminium alloy with a titanium top, supported by lenticular (aircraft) rods. To reduce her windage she had steel-wire sheets, and her winches, as well as all her crew except the helmsman, were stowed below deck. When Olin was asked if this would be the start of a new era in 8-Metres his reply was short: 'too much boat for too few berths'.

But *Iroquois* was not to have her race. Once the word was out, the defending Royal Canadian Yacht Club realised it had little chance of designing and building a boat with sufficient

ABOVE: *The crew on* Iroquois *works from a deep cockpit.*
BELOW: *A detail of the cabin top.*
OPPOSITE: *Olin Stephens, Honorary Chairman of the 2002 8-Metre World Cup in Helsinki. Between racing he enjoys sailing as a guest on board* Iroquois.

speed to stop *Iroquois* from snatching The Canada's Cup. The only solution appeared to be a change of rules. Thus, it happened: the RCYC adopted the less developed and more affordable two-ton class to be The Canada's Cup class. *Iroquois* was left stranded in a class of her own.

Van Voorhis soon learned *Iroquois* was an easy boat to handle but not quite so easy to drive fast. Olin and Rod were occasionally called in for a sail and, once the key to her performance was found, she proved to be an incredibly quick boat; so much so that to keep her from winning too much, her Canadian rivals asked that she trail buckets to slow her down; but even that could not stop her from taking a serious proportion of the silverware.

In 1983 *Iroquois* was shipped to Norway to participate in the 8-Metre World Cup hosted by the Royal Norwegian Yacht Club in honour of the 80th birthday of King Olav of Norway. Satisfying all the pundits she won, and, in 1984, continued her victory tour by winning the World Cup in Sandhamn, Sweden. In 1986 she was sold to a syndicate in Helsinki. *Iroquois* continues to race in events on both sides of the Atlantic to this day.

Her stunning performance triggered the building of some 15 modern Eights and the end is not in sight. Following the latest trends in the America's Cup the modern Eights are equipped with the best that money can buy and an active class association helps to provide the races that keep the fleets alive. So much for Olin's early dismissiveness! The legend of *Iroquois* lives on at the Granströms Batvårv in Hangö, Finland, where no expense is spared to keep her in immaculate racing trim.

PREVIOUS DOUBLE PAGE: Iroquois *driven hard during the 2002 World Cup in Helsinki. 25 knots of wind and big waves don't seem to bother her too much.*

ABOVE: Iroquois *sailing in Helsinki. Treadmaster decking provides good antislip for the crew.*

OPPOSITE: Iroquois *crosses in front of* Dora *on the windward leg.*

Through the past few decades, racing within the various Metre Classes has survived despite the swings in popularity. Of all the classes the 8-Metres have probably enjoyed the most loyal ownership. Ostensibly this is due to their ideal proportions: small enough to race with an amateur crew, yet large enough to be used for comfortable and swift coastal cruising; many 8-Metres have been treasured by the same families for generations. For decades active fleets have been kept together in countries such as Sweden, Finland, Canada, France, and the USA and in recent years the class has seen a large number of old boats restored to their former glory. The annual World Cup is usually attended by some 30 boats, all coming together to create a true spectacle of beauty and to forge lasting friendships.

The trophy that has the credit for bringing the Eights to the Great Lakes of North America is The Canada's Cup. Long known as the 'America's Cup of the Great Lakes' and the 'Blue Riband of fresh water', the heavily embossed silver trophy symbolises true match racing supremacy on the Great Lakes. The rivalry between the Rochester Yacht Club (RYC) of New York and the Royal Canadian Yacht Club (RCYC) flourished despite the days of the great depression and both yacht clubs went to extreme lengths in their efforts to win this prestigious trophy. In 1930 each club commissioned three Eights for Canada: *Quest* by Fife, *Vision* by Nicholson, *Norseman* by Roue. For the USA *Thisbe* was designed by Crane, *Cayuga* by Paine, and *Conewago* was designed by a 21-year-old man named Olin Stephens. Olin

had designed only a few boats by this time; indeed 'Connie' was design No 9. Walter Farley, skipper and head of the *Conewago* Syndicate, chose this young designer, impressed by the success of his 6-Metre design, *Thalia*. Nevertheless, it was something of a gamble to commission such a young and inexperienced man to design such an expensive yacht! Who could possibly have known that this young man would become one of the most successful naval architects of the Twentieth Century?

The selection of the defender was made after a gruelling series of eliminations. *Conewago* was first to drop out, the boat and her crew clearly lacking speed against those of the established designers. However, once The Canada's Cup was over, the young Olin Stephens was invited to take the tiller of his 'loser'. He steered 'Connie' to a surprising and incredibly easy win in the newly established 'George H. Gooderham Cup', beating the entire fleet of Eights, including those boats that had outmanoeuvred her in the trials. Not without justification, following these results *Conewago* was soon taken over from her original syndicate by the Rochester Yacht Club. It seemed that she could well be a very hard boat to beat after all. Following *Conewago*'s change of ownership she successfully defended The Canada's Cup in 1932 and 1934.

ABOVE: *Action on board the 8-Metres, hoisting the spinnakers at the windward mark.*

Nyala

Year of build	1938
S&S Design number	214
Builder	Henry Nevins,
	City Island, New York
First owner	Frederick T. Bedford
Length overall	21.35 m
Beam	3.6 m
Draft	2.67 m
Displacement	24,600 kg

Before the 12-Metres were chosen for the America's Cup competition, their numbers were limited. Displacing over 20 tons and demanding a well-trained crew of 11 able men, the racing in these yachts was restricted to an elite group of wealthy yachtsmen. To illustrate this fact one need only think of men like T.O.M. Sopwith and Harold Vanderbilt, who owned more than one J-Class and, in addition, commissioned a Twelve for more casual racing. Contrary to the 6- and 8-Metres, most 12-Metres were built after the war and the America's Cup certainly drove the naval architects to the very limits of the rating rules, making this the most developed fleet of all Metre classes. For 50 years the 12-Metres designed by Sparkman & Stephens were a reference point of technology and design. With only one exception, all the successful Twelves defending the America's Cup up to 1980 came from the S&S office. The most beautiful of all remain the pre-war racing stars, such as *Vim* and *Nyala*, both S&S designs that solidly hammered the fleets in Europe and the USA. After the war it was soon clear that the lines of these yachts would be hard to improve. Even 20 years after her launch, *Vim* showed a convincing clean pair of heels to all but one America's Cup yacht, but even *Columbia* found it was a serious struggle to beat the grand old lady of the Twelves.

TOP LEFT: *The 1938 aluminium coffee grinder survived the test of time.*
BELOW: Nyala*'s original wheel and binnacle.*
OPPOSITE: Nyala *at the America's Cup Jubilee, Cowes 2001.*
FOLLOWING DOUBLE PAGE: *With Torben Grael at the wheel,* Nyala *came first in class during the Jubilee Regatta in Cowes.*

The president of the Standard Oil Corporation, Frederick Bedford, commissioned *Nyala* as a wedding present for his daughter. During her early years, the fame of *Nyala* may have been overshadowed by the results of her sister *Vim* in Europe but her success was actually no less. Built shortly after Olin's first 12-Metre, *Northern Light*, *Nyala* was another S&S winner that came off the slipway of the great yard of Henry Nevins.

The 1939 season on the US east coast was *Nyala*'s as she grabbed just about all the silver there was to win. After the war Gerald W. Ford owned her for close to 30 years until she was wrecked in a hurricane. She was restored and continued a leisurely but successful racing career as one of the prettiest Twelves on the coast. In 1995 Mr. Patrizio Bertelli, head of the famous fashion house Prada in Italy, purchased *Nyala*. Taking her to Federico Nardi of Cantiere Navale dell'Argentario carte blanche was given to perform a restoration that would set the standard. She is still the most faithfully restored Twelve and *Nyala* rules the classic 12-Metre fleet in the Mediterranean. With top-notch helmsmen such as Torben Grael steering her around the cans and a selected team of Prada sailors to match, very few Twelves get even close enough to read the name on her transom.

In the best of traditional boatbuilding practices her hull was double planked using Honduras mahogany over Port Orford cedar. Double-planked hulls are durable, strong, and light, but also very expensive. The total thickness of the planking is the same as that of a traditionally planked hull; each layer being approximately half of the total. Little effort is required to bend the long thin planks, but this doesn't make the life of the builder any easier; on the contrary, the thin planks make it harder to obtain a perfectly fair hull. Only the very best yards were able to produce yachts with this method of construction. Double planking would give the owner a stiffer hull, more resistant to change of climate and, come rain or shine, the hull would remain watertight. Nevins had a world-class reputation for building fine yachts. The quality of their workmanship and materials was first-class and *Nyala* was no exception. Both Olin and Rod Stephens took a close interest in the design of efficient deck gear and, under their guidance, Nevins produced a full range of outstanding winches, tracks and other deck gear. For *Nyala*, S&S designed low-profile winches with large-diameter drums mounted on pedestals for swift and powerful operation. In 1938 the winches, cast in lightweight aluminium alloy, were state of the art. They provided a tremendous advantage in tacking duels as the fast and powerful winches could set the large overlapping genoas much faster than smaller traditional ones.

It was, in part, Federico Nardi's personal drive and enthusiasm in wanting to rebuild *Nyala* that resulted in Mr. Bertelli shipping her to the Cantiere Navale dell'Argentario. The project was enormous and the only demand was for perfection to the last detail. This included the correct use of originally specified materials; no adhesives were used and most planking under the waterline was replaced using the old technique with silicon-

OPPOSITE BOTTOM LEFT: *Close up of a beautiful piece of engineering.*
BOTTOM RIGHT: *Looking forward from the cockpit the flush deck has hardly any obstructions.*
ABOVE: Nyala *in her new home waters of Santo Stefano.*

bronze screws and wooden pegs. All bronze floors and knees were replaced and so were a good number of oak frames.

For the deck, only select quarter-sawn spruce with cotton caulking and black rubber seams was good enough. *Nyala* taught the yard much about the advantage of American boatbuilding, which, contrary to the European yards, did not employ steel frames or floors. This alone preserved much of the planking, as the corrosion of steel would be detrimental to timber. Not many of the original fittings had remained with the yacht, but the Sparkman & Stephens archives uncovered most of the drawings and each and every fitting was remade to these original drawings. No compromises to modern requirements were allowed and no cost was spared – even the old chain and gear arrangement was reconstructed for the primary winch and the pedestal was cast in aluminium.

Her interior of white pine is mostly original, and after the old varnish was scraped back most of it was refitted. The one compromise was in the mast, for which a copy of the 1939 aluminium mast of *Vim* was built rather than using the originally specified wooden spar of 1938.

ABOVE: Nyala, *a breathtaking beauty, sailing in style wherever she goes.*
LEFT: *Designed for racing round the cans, Nyala's galley was limited to the minimum allowed under the rule.*
OPPOSITE: *Below deck one has a clear view of the Port Orford cedar inner planking. Nevins fastened the planking with screws.*
FOLLOWING DOUBLE PAGE: *A view below looking forward. Nyala's light but strong construction is striking.*

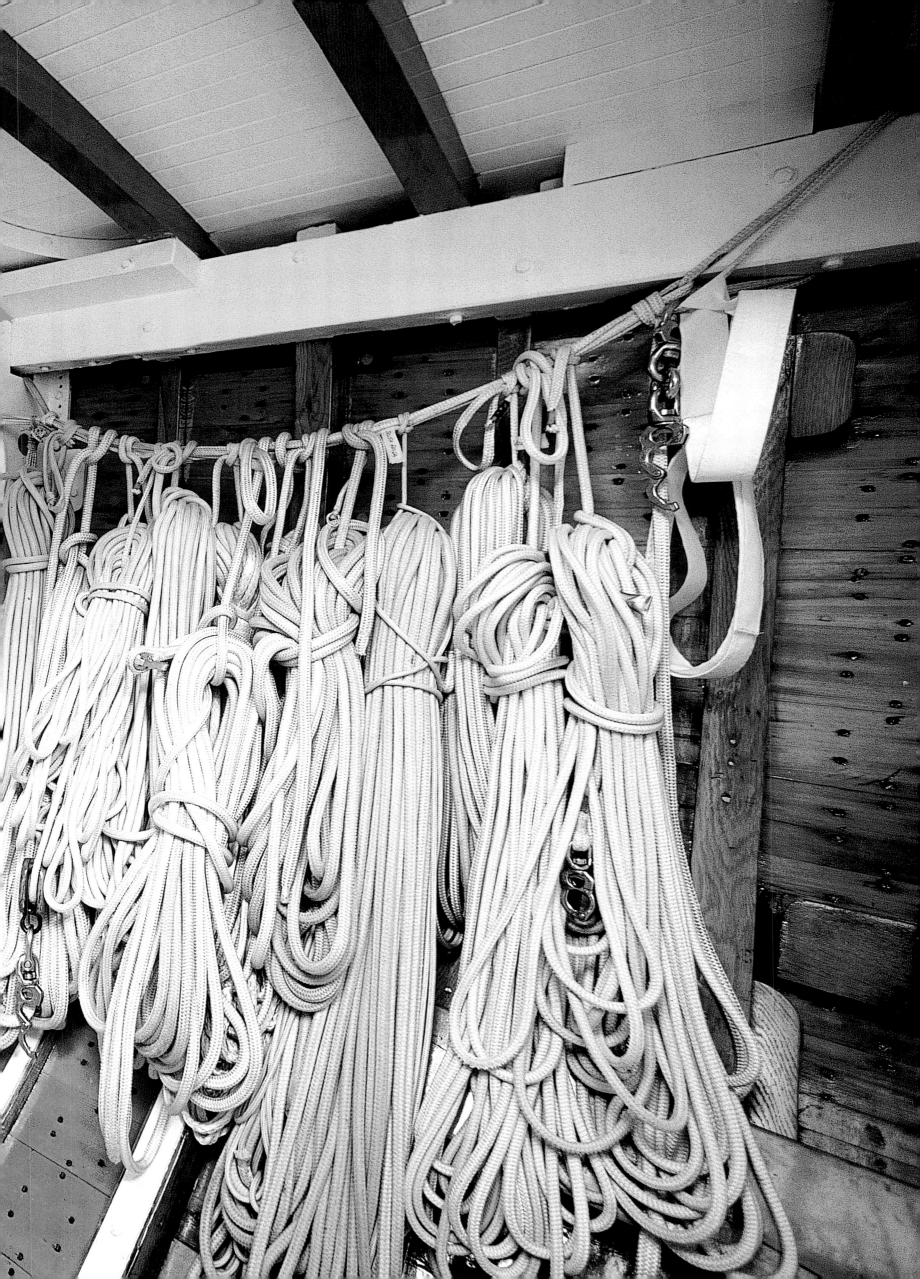

Vim

Year of build	1939
S&S Design number	279
Builder	Henry Nevins,
	City Island, New York
First owner	Harold S. Vanderbilt
Length overall	21.13 m
Beam	3.66 m
Draft	2.67 m
Displacement	28,490 kg

When it comes to classic 12-Metres the one name that stands out is surely *Vim*. For many years she remained Olin's best. After the 1937 America's Cup match, Harold Vanderbilt asked Sparkman & Stephens to design a 12-Metre to race in England. She was to be built at Nevins on City Island and would soon prove to be the yardstick by which other Twelves would be measured for decades to come.

Almost immediately after her launch *Vim* was shipped to England where a series of races 'around the coast' attracted excellent competition. In England it was T.O.M. Sopwith who countered Vanderbilt's assault with *Tomahawk*, a new Twelve designed by Charles Nicholson. However, despite the great genius of Nicholson, *Tomahawk* was barely a match for the American yacht. *Vim*'s record for the first season was 21 firsts out of 28 starts and she was never less than third.

Although to the untrained eye she differed little from the other Twelves, she was clearly a breakthrough. Much, if not all, of what Olin had learned to date was incorporated in *Vim*. What was felt to be wrong on earlier Twelves was corrected and methodically tank tested. Comparative calculations quantified the faults and merits and the rating rule was explored to its limits. Her rig was optimised with the best that money could buy.

TOP LEFT: *US15, the legendary Twelve, close to unbeatable for the best part of 20 years.*
LEFT AND OPPOSITE: Vim *at the 1991 Porto Cervo Veteran Boat Rally.*
FOLLOWING DOUBLE PAGE: Vim *at La Nioulargue, St. Tropez, 1994.*

During her first season in England it was clear that war loomed and, as the summer came to an end, *Vim* was shipped back to America. There she spent several years waiting in a cradle at the City Island boatyard until she was bought for a song by John Mathews. He found himself with a Twelve as good as new, with barely a season under her belt. After fitting a small engine and making some minor conversions below deck to add comfort, he happily campaigned her under the CCA Rule, but not for long. In 1957, when the deed of gift for the America's Cup was changed to the Twelves, a challenge was received from England. John suddenly realised that he owned a possible defender for the Cup and, at the time, *Vim* was the only Twelve around!

John spent the summer converting *Vim* back to her original racing trim. 'She goes like the Devil in light airs, she goes like the Devil when it blows, what could I change?' Despite her age and the knowledge that three new Twelves would be built for the defence of the Cup, John was determined that *Vim* would go to the ball. Totally passionate in his quest, he spared no expense in her refit and installed a complete new rig with the best sails, which for the first time were made of Dacron. Her competition came from the American home camp with *Weatherly* designed by Philip L. Rhodes, *Easterner* by C. Raymond Hunt, and her new S&S stable mate, *Columbia*.

Although *Vim* was regarded as the benchmark to which the performance of all the others would be measured, it still came as something of a shock that the old girl quickly eliminated *Weatherly* followed by *Easterner* in the trials. But if that was not enough, she won the first race and more than a few to follow against her newer sister *Columbia*!

Vim's skipper, Bus Mosbacher, should certainly take a lot of the credit for her stunning performance. He developed the team and boat-handling, perfecting the finest of details. Running with the spinnaker, they invented the 'dip pole' when gybing – this would become the standard on all Twelves and other big boats for decades to come. Competition remained close, so close that a final trial was held between *Columbia* and *Vim*. Ultimately good old *Vim* could no longer hold out against her younger sister, losing by the narrowest possible margin. *Columbia* was selected as the 17th defender for the America's Cup.

But *Vim*'s role was far from over. In 1962 she was shipped to Australia to serve as a trial horse for *Gretel*, the first of a new generation of challengers. Finally, in 1983 after nearly 20 years, the men from down under snatched the Cup from its pedestal at the New York Yacht Club.

In the Nineties *Vim*'s life was to come full circle. The owner of her first opponent, *Tomahawk*, bought and lovingly restored *Vim* in Italy to rejoin the old sparring partners for a new round of competition with the Mediterranean fleet.

ABOVE AND LEFT: *Getting ready to set the kite.*
RIGHT: Vim *off Porto Cervo, Sardinia, for the Veteran Boat Rally in* *1991.*

6-Metres

In 1921, Olin and Rod arrived back at the Larchmont Yacht Club after a cold and rainy day's sail on a leaky family boat. Longing for a warm shower and dry clothes, they agreed they would not go back on a boat that day even if paid to. At that moment the eminent yachtsman Sherman Hoyt walked in the shower room. 'We need crew to sail our two new 6-Metres, any takers?' Without a moment's hesitation Olin and Rod jumped back into their soaking wet gear. It was their first opportunity to get a sail in these fine racing boats. They were immediately enamoured and later convinced their father to do away with the family cruising boat and buy an old Six named *Natka*.

Natka had not been overly successful and could be bought at a reasonable price, giving the two young brothers ample opportunity to learn more about the secrets of the class. They won the occasional trophy and thoroughly enjoyed the class racing on Long Island Sound. Many of the best sailors then raced 6-Metres, and being part of the events gave the Stephens boys the opportunity to become acquainted with men who could teach them a thing or two. They were introduced to the likes of Cornelius Shields, Ted Hood, Brigs Cunningham, Sherman Hoyt and many other great sailors.

It would not be long before Olin would design his first Six. Much to his delight, his design was published in *Yachting* as a '6-Metre with possibilities'. The enquiries slowly rolled in. The first 6-Metre to be built to Olin's design was *Thalia* and, while she was not the quickest boat, the local fleet recognised the potential of her young creator. Often supported by Clinton Crane's recommendation, more orders followed and Olin was able to correct some of his thinking in subsequent boats. His fourth Six, *Cherokee*, won the class championships and established his name for good.

The 6-Metres were much more affordable than Eights or Twelves and a failing experimental design would not necessarily ruin her owner. In this class, gambling on new ideas has always been part of the game but the performance gap between the boats has remained marginal. The older boats remain in the fleet and provide great racing for a fraction of the money that the top boat owners spend.

The adoption of the Metre Rule in 1927 by the American Yachting Association gave a tremendous boost to intercontinental competition. Trophies such as the Seawanhaka Cup and the British America's Cup provided exciting new venues for the 6-Metres. Loaded on board freighters the Americans would often cross the Atlantic to race their counterparts on the other side of the pond. The established European designers may have had a 20-year lead but, once the two continents met, it was soon clear that the conservative British approach to yacht design did not always produce boats that were able to keep up with the methodically designed shapes from the board of a 25-year-old man.

There was more to it than the hulls alone: as a talented and observant sailor, Olin often drove the boats himself while his brother Rob developed an expert eye for the rig and spreader arrangements. The American boats also had an extensive sail wardrobe covering a full range of weather conditions.

The British boats initially did not fancy the overlapping genoa jib. The genoa jib was a sail developed on the Six Metres and resulted in a breakthrough in performance. The Italian 6-Metre *Cora IV* experimented with the overlapping jib as early as 1925 and first used it during Genoa Week in 1926. In 1927, again during Genoa Week, the Swedish Six, *Maybe*, owned by the famous Metre-boat family Salén, took a large flat-cut reaching jib and sheeted it in when going to windward. The result was an outright victory, and the genoa was established. Although at the time there was no clear understanding why the sail worked so well, the result was convincing and yachtsmen subsequently converted to the larger sail.

The class rules had no provision for the new sail, as only the fore-triangle was measured. After a long debate at the 1927 IYRU Conference it was decided not to make a rule change to limit the length of the foot and to leave the measurement instructions for headsails unchanged. It is interesting to note that all represented countries took a great interest in the new development. That is, all but one: Great Britain stated that British yachtsmen 'showed no interest at all in the use of these large headsails or so called *Genoa Jibs*'. But, since they could not see how the genoa could contribute to or harm the competition, they would go along with whatever Professor Ljungberg and Johan Anker recommended.

Before the 12-Metres were used for the America's Cup, most development in Metre boats came from the 6-Metre Class. The best example is the all time star 6-Metre, *Goose*. This 1938 design proved to be a breakthrough, a consistent winner and certainly the best pre-war 6-Metre in the world. Her lines led to the 12-Metre *Vim* and 8-Metre *Iskareen*, which would both become icons in their class. In the following years the new Metre-boat designs would be refined but would only perform marginally better.

The next real step forward came in 1966 with the 12-Metre *Intrepid*. The situation was now reversed, a breakthrough S&S 12-Metre design would lead to the 6-Metre *Toogooloowoo IV* and the 8-Metre *Iroquois*. Between 1928 and 1986 Sparkman & Stephens designed close to 30 6-Metres. Many of Olin's 6-Metre designs are among the class favourites today, the affection seems mutual.

OPPOSITE: *6-Metres have always been close to Olin's heart. The class is very much alive still today. Here are three Sixes battling it out on the downwind leg of the 1999 Régates Royales.*

Offshore Yachts

The majority of yachts designed by Olin Stephens had off-shore capabilities and, with over 2,500 designs, any selection based on success, cruising ability, or beauty would inevitably be incomplete. Covering over 50 years of active design, yachts from his board won every notable ocean race at least once. It makes one wonder what was the secret of his success; it had to be more than just the genius mind that so often is quoted. To maintain success in an ever-changing world, the multitude of challenges faced requires more than dry brainpower. Through their personal experience and success in offshore racing, Olin and Rod Stephens shared a deep respect for the sea, which led to an ever-returning quest for safety and seaworthiness. Maybe the lack of formal education stimulated a profound interest in applied scientific research, which in turn led to a deeper understanding of fluid dynamics and the parameters that influenced the motion of a hull at sea.

Olin's devotion to finding a workable rating system with which yachts of different sizes, shapes, and speeds could fairly race one another made him a valued member of most significant rule committees on both sides of the Atlantic. The constant inter-action between development in yacht design and their governing rules helped to define the influence and weight of both isolated

and combined parameters, the numbers that shaped the hull and balanced drive and drag. The creative brainpower of naval architects around the world would tirelessly seek for the opening in the rules that would lead to a winning design and a moment of glory until the rule committee revised the formula, often creating new hidden and unintended openings.

Being at the heart of the committees and their Research and Development efforts, Olin had the opportunity to observe and learn more with each apparent flaw that surfaced. Today computers allow complex scoring of race results at modestly equipped yacht clubs and, with IMS, competition is probably fairer than ever. Still, it is safe to say that there will never be a perfect rating rule. Nor should there be, for without the imperfect rule the drive for competitive development would, inevitably, diminish. Olin Stephens never retired from that greatest of all games in yachting and, at 90, he committed

himself to work on a Velocity Prediction Programme for sails.

Throughout his active career at S&S, Olin never left the stage and was able consistently to deliver yachts with winning capabilities under a wide range of conditions. As new building materials emerged and rating rules changed, the basics for S&S offshore designs stood firm: good sailing characteristics and speed, hulls built tight and sound. As expert ocean skippers, both Olin and Rod Stephens had experienced firsthand the comfort of a dry bunk at the end of a watch; barometers would indicate the weather but could not turn the storm. Offshore yachts designed by S&S were strong, improving performance through science, while commonsense and intuition avoided extremes. The building survey was often part of the package supplied, controlling the quality and seaworthiness of the boats that carried the signature of Sparkman & Stephens. Rod was a sincere and dedicated critic who had to be satisfied; he was highly influential in maintaining the best standards.

THIS PAGE: Bolero, *a legendary S&S offshore yacht, photographed at the Antigua Classic Series in 1996.*

Bolero

Year of build	1949
S&S Design number	711
Builder	Henry Nevins, City Island, New York
First owner	Commodore John Nicholas Brown
Length overall	22.40 m
Length waterline	15.54 m
Beam	4.85 m
Draft	2.90 m
Displacement	42,000 kg

In 1949 when Commodore John Nichols Brown of the New York Yacht Club approached S&S he knew what he was looking for: a grand sea boat designed to take the maximum advantage of the rating rules, to race and cruise him successfully across the seven seas. The starting point was *Baruna*, a well known 1937 S&S design with similar characteristics. The result was *Bolero*; certainly one of the most beautiful wooden maxis ever built. Beauty came with speed to match and her success was exceptional. As Queen of the New York Yacht Club fleet she not only captured the hearts of many sailors but also a string of impressive victories including a first out of 89 starters in the 1956 Bermuda Race. She is a magnificent yacht that exemplifies S&S's ability to find a healthy balance between speed, seaworthiness, comfort, and beauty.

As with many other famous S&S yachts, the lines of *Bolero* were trusted to the yard of Henry Nevins on City Island, NY. Olin Stephens was pleased to see Mr. Nevins build *Bolero*, knowing they could achieve the highest standards to satisfy the expectations of Commodore Brown, a man who left no room for compromises. As one of the first post-war Maxis she

TOP LEFT: Bolero*'s steering position.*
BELOW: *The forward hatch leads down to the crew's quarters.*
OPPOSITE: Bolero *roaring along with eased sheets at the Antigua Classic Series in 1996.*
FOLLOWING DOUBLE PAGE: Bolero*'s power and beauty has seldom been matched in offshore design.*

incorporated the latest development in yacht construction. At the mast step, and extending well forward, she featured a Monel-web-frame-structure, so distributing the loads of the mast as well as two 'coffee grinders' amidships and a balancing centreboard. So different from today's flat-out ocean racers, she was built with a lavish interior, two state rooms, a large main cabin, separate crew quarters and a well-equipped galley to accommodate the crew of 12 in style and comfort.

Cornelius Shields, an eminent yachtsman, was regularly put in charge, later making his mark in the America's Cup. A small group of dedicated sailors and friends were often invited on board for the major races, with Olin Stephens and Professor Ken Davidson joining as watch captains. Olin and Ken Davidson had been long time friends, together pioneering tank testing and running countless models of S&S designs through the Hoboken tank. As an excellent celestial navigator, Ken Davidson would always be assigned that role when he was on board.

Throughout her racing career, the boat that would give *Bolero* her stiffest competition was her older sister *Baruna*. Whenever these two great S&S designs met, the encounter would provide the closest of racing. Take the Newport–Annapolis

RIGHT: *Natural ventilation:* Dorade *vents and sturdy but elegant skylights.*
OPPOSITE: Bolero *on a reach in a fresh breeze. Try to keep up with that!*

race, 1951: with 32 entries this winter ocean race was well attended, and should anyone believe that close offshore racing is the sole custody of today's events, then *Bolero* and *Baruna* proved otherwise. Throughout the 466-mile race they never lost sight of each other, often racing within a boat's length. When the breeze dropped *Baruna* had a slight edge, and as it filled in again *Bolero* would pull ahead.

Olin was watch captain on *Bolero* and the excitement was tremendous when, after 466 miles of concentrated racing, *Baruna* crossed the line first a mere 24 seconds ahead of *Bolero*. Conditions had been light and it took five days for all 32 boats to finish.

Today *Bolero* is still going strong. An extensive restoration in 1995 has secured her future for generations to come. Wherever the wind may take her, *Bolero* will make heads turn as one of the most elegant S&S creations ever.

TOP LEFT: *Powerful Lewmar self-tailing winches help control the sails with a modest crew.*
TOP RIGHT: *The vang controls the boom and keeps the mainsail working on every course.*
RIGHT: *A powerered windlass on the foredeck.*
OPPOSITE TOP: *Racing the oceans in style.* Bolero *has a spacious and luxurious interior.*
BELOW: Bolero *on her way in after a day's racing off Antigua.*

Finisterre

Year of build	1954
S&S Design number	1054
Builder	Seth Persson, Saybrook, Connecticut
First owner	Carleton Mitchell
Length overall	11.73 m
Length waterline	8.38 m
Beam	3.43 m
Draft	1.19 m
Displacement	10,129 kg

Small enough for singlehanded day sailing, comfortable enough for grand cruising, able enough to cross the oceans, fast enough to win races, and large enough to hold luxury features such as a mechanical refrigerator. A centreboard boat with the shallow draft for shoal-water cruising in Chesapeake Bay while her ample beam would provide the stability for extended ocean passages. Her name was to be *Finisterre* and the concept 'to have your cake and eat it'. When Carleton Mitchell ('Mitch') walked into the office of Sparkman & Stephens with his design criteria, it seemed a mission impossible. Olin Stephens must have been hesitant. Apart from the apparent dichotomy of characteristics he was always concerned about safety at sea and therefore never really fancied centreboarders for offshore racing – they could capsize and turn over with no hope of coming back. Furthermore Mitch had published his ideas and objectives in magazine articles, exposing his project to public scrutiny.

TOP LEFT: Finisterre *was considered too small for wheel steering, but it worked out just fine.*
BELOW: *The main hatch leading down to the cabin accommodation.*
OPPOSITE: Finisterre *reflects beautifully in the waters off Trieste.*
NEXT DOUBLE PAGE: Finisterre *gliding through the Marano Lagunare channels on the Adriatic.*

Luckily *Finisterre* turned out to be anything but a failure and became a true legend of yachting. Mitch's initial goal was to have a floating home that would sail well, a flat-out racer was never in the equation and her rating was not even part of the discussion during the design process. Mitch spent more time thinking about the smallest detail and selected materials and equipment with great care. He needed to sail and race the oceans in comfort.

Her list of gear and gadgets would have done justice to a maxi: a belt-driven ice-maker, a coal stove, a Swiss hand-crank record player, a German FM player, and four Warfdale speakers. On deck the tiller had to make way for a wheel, which was, perhaps, rather unusual for a 38 ft boat, but so much more

suitable for the autopilot. She also had a prototype wind indicator in the cockpit. In a way, *Finisterre* was a 38 ft boat with 72 ft boat's equipment.

The yard of Seth Persson from Old Saybrook, a one-man shop, took great pride in his work and craftsmanship. With *Finisterre* he had the opportunity to use the best materials

OPPOSITE TOP LEFT: *A small coal stove keeps things comfortable below when it is not so warm on deck.*
BOTTOM LEFT: *The crank to lift the centreboard.*
BOTTOM RIGHT: *The galley.*
ABOVE: *The main saloon.* Finisterre *is spacious for a boat of her size.*

money could buy; she was double planked in Honduras mahogany on Port Orford cedar with white-oak frames. Her mast step was in Monel and her floors were in bronze. For her interior a complete mock-up was built to check that the drawings had not hidden any inconveniences. *Finisterre* was among the first boats to have their sails cut in new synthetic fibres such as Dacron.

With her generous beam, low ballast and shallow draft she sailed straight through an opening in the rating rules. But her favourable rating was not the only reason for her outstanding success. Mitch, a great ocean-racing skipper, would drive his floating home hard. Always having a capable and hard-working crew on board, he was quoted as saying, 'Why spend all that money on fancy equipment to save a few seconds and then put a man on the wheel who gives away minutes'.

Finisterre's success was beyond anyone's expectations, winning the Bermuda Race three consecutive times, including the 1960 race which was sailed in truly big-boat weather with gales up to Force 9. *Bolero* set the course record but little *Finisterre* set the record on corrected time, outsailing 109 out of 135 starters without calling on handicap. *Finisterre* holds an amazing and unsurpassed record of victories, but still her owner would say that his boat was even more successful as a cruising boat.

Finisterre shook up the yachting world and she was followed by a whole range of carbon copies, near replicas and developments. Sparkman & Stephens designed a good number

for clients wanting to cruise and race in comfort. However, none matched the outstanding performance of the original. Centreboard boats would not always perform well in light weather, but neither did *Finisterre* after Mitch sold her. He clearly took a good part of the credit for the yacht's success. Mitch and his crew were able to recognise and take the luck when it crossed their path and with excellent seamanship they sailed *Finisterre* to fame.

Enjoying her retirement from active racing, *Finisterre* found a new home in the Adriatic Sea near Trieste. Her owner sails her year round and she enters an occasional race or rally. When she does, her crew will always be reminded that there has only been one *Finisterre* in the history of ocean racing.

ABOVE: Finisterre *sailing gently along. Her days of intense offshore campaigns are over.*

Ice Fire

Year of build	1936
S&S Design number	125 Hull #3
Type	New York Yacht Club 32
Builder	Henry Nevins,
	City Island, New York
First owner	Ralph Manny
Length overall	13.82 m
Length waterline	9.75 m
Beam	3.23 m
Draft	1.98 m
Displacement	11,120 kg

In 1936 when a group of prominent members of the NYYC felt it was time to look for a successor to the Nathanael Herreshoff-designed New York Thirties, a cooperation between Sparkman & Stephens and the yard of Henry Nevins was judged as the favourite. Their NY32 would prove to be a worthy replacement for the much-loved Herreshoff boats. The S&S design had beautiful lines with moderate overhangs, although forward the overhangs were more pronounced than on the real offshore racers such as *Stormy Weather*.

The 7/8 rig was modern but, as with most features on the boat, there was no radical departure from what had previously been tried and tested.

The NY32 was the first real production design by S&S and, thanks to the well thought-through building method, the contract for building 20 identical boats was completed within five months. Saving construction time, the yard adopted the same methods used by Herreshoff 30 years before. Rather unusually, the hulls were built upside down and, once the hull was finished, it would be turned over to be fitted out. Despite the

TOP LEFT: Ice Fire *cruising with eased sheets.*
CENTRE: *The helmsman's domain: tiller and main sheet.*
BOTTOM: Ice Fire *has her companionway in an unusual place.*
OPPOSITE: *To windward in the Adriatic.*
FOLLOWING DOUBLE PAGE: Ice Fire *competing for the Trophy Citta di Trieste in 2000.*

serial production, Nevins did not compromise on materials or craftsmanship. The planking was of fine Philippine mahogany on white-oak frames with Everdur fastenings. To save cost as well as weight, the deck was of Port Orford cedar covered with canvas. Assuring exclusivity, the NYYC agreed with Nevins that the mould would be destroyed after the last boat was completed.

Compared to her predecessor, the NY32 would be a more practical boat. Her moderate sail area would make her much easier for a short-handed crew and the separate double stateroom aft of the companionway gave some privacy so the ladies could come along for a sail as well. The forecastle was equipped with a separate head and pipe cot to accommodate the paid hand.

The galley was also forward so the hand could easily prepare the meals – such were the demands of those days. The NY32 soon proved to be a worthy successor of the much loved NY Thirty, and was equally well suited to the Bermuda Race or racing round the buoys. Just two months after the launch, *Apache* (hull no 2) won the Bermuda Race in her class.

The 20 identical boats provided the finest racing but equally pleased their owners in coastal events, gathering an exceptional number of victories. Rod Stephens bought a NY32 and considered her among his all-time favourites. For 23 years he thoroughly enjoyed racing and cruising *Mustang*. With the exception of hull no 8, which was lost in a fire, all NY32s have survived. *Ice Fire* is one of them and a fine example of the class. These boats brought the pleasure of owning a pretty and sensible good all-round boat, as well as the pride of owning such an undisputed all-time S&S classic.

ABOVE TOP: Ice Fire, *a strong racing contender as well as a great cruising boat.*
ABOVE: *The wash basin in the head.*
OPPOSITE TOP: *The galley with a gimballed cooker and oven.*
BELOW: *The main saloon is beautifully laid out – suitable for weekend sailing as well as long haul passages.*
FOLLOWING DOUBLE PAGE: Ice Fire *steaming along at hull speed.*

Kialoa II

Year of build	1963
S&S Design number	1713
Builder	Yacht Dynamics, Harbour City
First owner	John B. Kilroy
Length overall	22.40 m
Length waterline	17.22 m
Beam	4.55 m
Draft	3.58 m
Displacement	49,786 kg

For John B. (Jim) Kilroy, *Kialoa II* was the start of 25 years of offshore Maxi racing. *Kialoa II* and her crew of 24 would race every possible event around the globe. *Kialoa II* did well, taking honours in most of the offshore races at least once during her active racing career, including the 1971 Sidney-to-Hobart in gruelling conditions.

Jim Kilroy commissioned *Kialoa* with just one goal: to win. His approach left no room for compromise but ample for innovation. Most striking was the desire to build her in aluminium and the project was to be the largest of its kind in the USA at that time. The yard bestowed with this project was Yacht Dynamics whose management, Bud Gardiner, Ken Watts and Donald Douglas of the Douglas Aircraft Corporation, were all actively interested in boats and sailing. *Kialoa II* would not only bring advances through the use of aluminium but the computer lofting was also the first of its kind used in yacht building.

Douglas Aircraft had pioneered computer fairing in aircraft wings and fuselages and used the new software for fairing *Kialoa*'s hull. Aluminium was an advance in boatbuilding

TOP LEFT: Kialoa *has 3 wheels; one for the rudder, one for the trimtab and one to lock the two. Despite her size, she steers like a dinghy.*
BELOW: *Familiar on S&S offshore boats, Dorade vents.*
OPPOSITE: Kialoa II, *a powerful boat with a sleek rig and clean wake.*
NEXT DOUBLE PAGE: Kialoa *40 years on, and again the way she was.*

technology and by involving the science of aircraft design the learning curve was significantly shortened.

Kialoa's design was one of the first yachts to be equipped with a Radar Range Oven (known today as a microwave), which, combined with two large freezers, made life easy for the cook. Saving weight, balanced with the wish for comfort at sea, resulted in panelling made of light-weight material, the fine varnished-teak ceilings maintaining the feel of comfort and luxury. Accommodation below deck included three heads and two showers. What a difference compared with the standards of today's flat-out offshore racers, where the accommodation is hardly worth mentioning and anything related to comfort at sea appears to be a crime.

Originally built as a sloop, *Kialoa II* was converted to a yawl in 1968. At that time a separate rudder was installed aft and the original rudder was converted to a trimtab – being a development from the America's Cup 12-Metre *Intrepid*. The shortened boom worked better in rough sea conditions, and the mizzen was not counted in the rated sail area, giving that extra bit of flexibility. In this configuration she set numerous course records around the world until Jim Kilroy retired her in 1973 for his next boat, the S&S-designed *Kialoa III*. This *Kialoa* was also highly successful, setting and holding the record from Sydney to Hobart for 19 years.

With red-shirted crews and his personal sailnumber 13131, Jim Kilroy's boats would tirelessly campaign around the globe for the best part of 25 years. When he was asked whether maxi yachting was a rich man's sport he said: 'Certainly not, on board

there's only one rich man and there's twenty five poor, they enjoy it more than the rich man does.'

In 1984 Frank and Cynthia Robben bought a very tired *Kialoa II* and started the first major refit. Cruising the world for 15 years, *Kialoa II* became their home until they reluctantly put her up for sale in Honolulu in 1999. Dutch yachtsman Jos Fruytier bought her and, after cruising the Pacific with his family, he decided to sail the yacht to Turkey for a major overhaul. At Metur Yachts in Bodrum, a two-year uncompromising refit programme started.

The aluminium hull was completely stripped inside and out, checked for corrosion and coated with a new paint system. Since the interior was removed the opportunity was also taken to replace all electrical systems as well as generators. Retaining the original styling with white panelling and varnished teak, the interior was renovated and brought up to the rigorous standards of today. On deck the hardware was updated, all standing and running rigging was renewed, and a full wardrobe of sails was built.

When she ran down the slipway in May 2002 *Kialoa II* was as good as new and she's a good example that not just the wooden classics deserve such extensive restorations. Quality designs such as *Kialoa II* are the next generation of classics. They offer excellent sailing and have a strong appeal to the real sailors who enjoy cruising the world in comfort and speed. Maybe the life of a maxi also begins at 40.

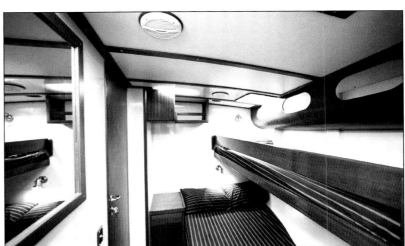

OPPOSITE TOP: *The McDonnell Douglas roots are clearly evident in the functional lightweight interior.* Kialoa *sleeps 12 in comfort.*
BELOW: *The magic of the gimballed tray mounted on the galley bar. It works in the worst of weathers; if* Kialoa *heels, this tray keeps the wine in the glasses and dinner on the plates.*
TOP: Kialoa *moves effortlessly with the wind and waves.*
ABOVE: *In the cabins* Kialoa *feels like a spacious floating airliner.*
NEXT DOUBLE PAGE: *Sea trials on the Aegean. There's no stopping her: the chase boat did 16 knots and* Kialoa *just left it behind.*

Swans

Early one morning in 1966, Rod Stephens awaited the arrival of a Finnish acquaintance in the lobby of a Helsinki hotel. The Finn was eager to start a production boatyard specialising in quality sailing yachts and, familiar with the long tradition of fine boatbuilding in Finland, Rod had often contemplated such an idea. But the man he was about to meet was not a sailor, nor did he have any experience building boats. Testing his devotion, Rod told him he was very busy and that he could only meet him at 5.30 a.m. Pekka Koskenkyla arrived punctually and the two men sat down to exchange ideas. Mr. Koskenkyla owned a plot of land up north in Pietersaari and dreamed of starting a yard, employing jobless furniture makers in the area. Willing to support the dream, Rod decided to give it a go. After discussing several designs, the men opted to start with a slightly modified design based on the proven S&S *Hestia*. The design and layout would be standardised and made ready for production.

Thus Nautor was established and, in a makeshift shed, the first Swan 36 was built. Despite their efforts and good intentions, the result was disappointing. Olin's first inspection in England led to a long list of deficiencies. At that time S&S was working on a 43 ft design for Koskenkyla's compatriot, Ake Lindquist. When Ake visited the S&S office, the idea of building his boat at Nautor was discussed. Being a Lloyd's surveyor, he felt that he could handle the very evident problem – the new company knew little about boats. He could watch and oversee the work and get a good boat at reasonable cost. Still it would take a while before the yard reached the level of quality that would establish their reputation.

Around the same time the management of America's most prestigious yard, Palmer Johnson, came to the office of S&S. Palmer Johnson had recognised a niche in the market for medium to large production offshore sailing yachts and was

exploring possible designs and, indeed, a yard. The men from Palmer Johnson discussed their ideas with Olin and Rod. Nautor came in the picture – they could build the boats at a very attractive price and Ake's 43 ft boat was the ideal prototype for a new range of designs. Palmer Johnson liked the concept and granted Nautor a first order for 24(!) Swan 43 ft yachts. An obviously excited Pekka Koskenkyla headed for the Finnish government which was ready to support this young venture with a loan, enabling them to build a state-of-the-art production boatyard. Nautor now had to master fibreglass construction too. The quality problems still had to be overcome and Rod would engage his expertise training boatbuilders, gradually working them up to building sound and seaworthy yachts. As a surveyor for Lloyd's, Ake Lindquist was able to guide the young Nautor yard to a consistent level of quality as required for Lloyd's 100 A1 standards. After the initial problems were overcome, the yard would continue to improve standards and their Swans would become synonymous for the finest-quality production yachts in the world.

Sparkman & Stephens continued to design a range of Swans from 36 ft to 76 ft in length and established that unmistakable Swan look. A beautifully balanced hull with a low wedge-shaped cabin top blending naturally with the camber of the deck. The yachts were finished with carefully laid teak decks and hand-rubbed rails, enhancing the already distinguished looks. Rod Stephens would often travel to Finland to oversee the work and ensure the yachts were built to withstand the toughest offshore conditions. At first the Swans appeared as beautiful cruising yachts but, in the hands of capable sailors, they soon turned out to be boats to watch in any offshore race. They harvested their share of the silver, participating in the Admiral's Cup, the Fastnet, Bermuda, Sidney–Hobart. A highlight was certainly the 1973–74 Whitbread Round the World Race when the Swan 65, *Sayula II*, convincingly won a hard-fought race.

The co-operation between Nautor and Sparkman & Stephens finally came to an end and, after several buy-outs, Nautor is now part of the British yard, Camper & Nicholson, which in turn is owned by an Italian investment company. Today Nautor's emphasis has changed from quality production boats to large custom-built sailing yachts. Close to 650 Swans sailed the Nautor yard to fame, and the yachts' prestige remains unquestioned, as do their speed and comfort at sea.

THIS PAGE: *Swans gather for the Swan Cup at Porto Cervo.*

PREVIOUS DOUBLE PAGE: Garuda, *a Swan 76 that sails the Seven Seas all year round. Here she is at the 1992 Rolex Swan World Cup.*
LEFT: Alitea, *a Swan 65, making her way down the windward leg at the Swan World Cup in Porto Cervo in 1996.*
ABOVE TOP: Xargo III, *a Swan 65 at Porto Cervo in 1980.*
ABOVE: Desperado, *another Swan 65. They have proved to be such excellent offshore yachts.*

TOP LEFT: *A beautiful helicopter shot of Swan 57* Seilan II.
BELOW: Indigo Bianco, *another Swan 57, participating in the 1998 Swan World Cup off the coast of Sardinia.*
ABOVE: Yellow Drama *dousing her spinnaker.*
RIGHT: Yellow Drama *sailing to windward.*
FAR RIGHT: Mitralis, *a Swan 57, at the Swan World Cup in 1992.*

The Swan 48 was one of the most popular Swans. They combined excellent sailing qualities with a timeless beauty that appealed to a wide public.

TOP: Full Pelt *sailing at Porto Cervo in 1998.*

MIDDLE: C'est la Vie *at Porto Cervo in 1992.*

ABOVE: Seilan, *also at Porto Cervo in 1986.*

OPPOSITE: *Harald Baum driving his* Elan *off Porto Cervo under spinnaker, a study of power and grace.* Elan *is actively campaigned and is one of those highly successful Swans.*

OPPOSITE: Cristina, *a Swan 41. These fine yachts also handsomely collected their share of the silver.*

TOP: Djata, *a Swan 47, with her crew riding the rail under the Mediterranean sun.*

MIDDLE: Lapalaton, *a Swan 43. Another successful member of the S&S family of Swans.*

ABOVE: *Swan 44* Blue Ithaca *under spinnaker on a close reach.*

America's Cup Yachts

The America's Cup, the oldest trophy in the history of sport, and the symbol of match-racing supremacy, started life as a 100-guinea trophy, offered as a prize by the Royal Yacht Squadron for the annual Squadron regatta. The schooner *America* won this trophy in 1851 and took it back to New York. In 1857 the owners presented it to the New York Yacht Club with a deed of gift, making it 'perpetually a challenge cup for friendly competition between foreign countries'.

In the 150 years after the schooner from the New World captured *The Auld Mug*, the prestige it represented was the only thing at stake. Win or lose, the only constant would be the staggering expense to compete, and the once friendly competition between nations came to be the contest of the absolute elite of yachting backed by almost-military campaigns and extraordinary budgets. The skippers were the most able of their time and had to withstand the pressure of performing. The naval architects who designed the yachts were selected for their innovative brilliance. In Europe George Watson pioneered scientific tank testing as early as 1899; his exhaustive research into fluid dynamics was privately funded and the results would be guarded rather than shared. His designs would counter those of the great Nathanael Herreshoff. But, however advanced the yachts and science behind the design, no method was ever found to tank test the skippers that sailed them.

The magic of the J-Class led to arguably the most beautiful racing yachts in history. Charles E. Nicholson designed all three British challengers for Sir Thomas Lipton and T.O.M. Sopwith. Nathanael Herreshoff passed the torch to W. Starling Burgess.

The design of one of these great yachts was the start of a life commitment to the America's Cup for Olin Stephens. In 1934 it was widely acknowledged that Charles Nicholson's *Endeavour* was faster than Starling Burgess's *Rainbow* and that the latter had won only through superior sailing. Defeat was coming ever closer and Harold Vanderbilt realised that unless ideas were drastically changed, the Americans would lose the Cup to the next challengers. He decided to ask Olin and Starling Burgess to cooperate and the result was *Ranger*.

Her dominant performance was so obvious that it took just seven starts for *Ranger* to be selected as the defender. *Endeavour II* never imposed a threat and *Ranger* went down in history as the fastest sloop ever built. *Ranger* was the first America's Cup experience for Olin and Rod Stephens. Rod proved himself as a valuable member of the crew. Charles Nicholson once said: 'We can turn out good hulls in England, but we have nobody to match Rod Stephens in rigging and organising them.' Rod would be on board every S&S defender until *Intrepid*. Olin served as *Ranger*'s afterguard and relief helmsman and would continue that role until *Constellation*. After the war the J-Class would be replaced by the more economic 12-Metre Class and this became the era of S&S dominance in America's Cup design. Until 1980 Olin would be responsible for all but one successful defending design.

Although the day-to-day office of Sparkman and Stephens produced a wide variety of yachts, America's Cup design would play a central role in Olin's life. Each challenge gave the chance for new ideas to be tested and further research to be carried out. No other event in sailing had more exposure and each successful S&S defender would reconfirm S&S's position as the world's leading naval architects. The knowledge gained with each defence went into the concept and detail of hundreds of S&S yachts, advancing the office and giving their owners around the world the joy of good cruising and successful racing.

THIS PAGE: *Two 12-Metres crossing tacks. The America's Cup stands for the closest yacht racing. There is no second, no excuse to lose.*

Columbia

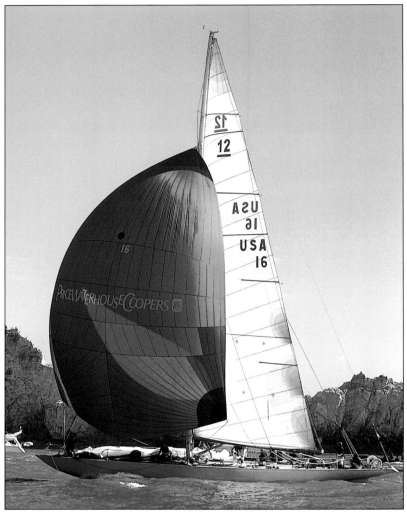

Year of build	1979
S&S Design number	1343
Builder	Nevins Yacht Yard, City Island, New York
First owner	Sears-Cunningham Syndicate
Length overall	21.15 m
Length waterline	13.93 m
Beam	3.55 m
Draft	2.73 m
Displacement	28,805 kg

The days of the great J-Boats were over. They had become too big, too expensive, too impractical. But the rules of the America's Cup called for the J-Class. Commodore Henry Sears of the New York Yacht Club believed the oldest trophy in sport should not be allowed to die and, in 1955, he travelled to England to meet Sir Ralph Gore, Commodore of the Royal Yacht Squadron. After receiving assurance from the Squadron that, in the event of a rule change, a 12-Metre would be built to challenge for the Cup, Commodore Sears negotiated the alteration of the deed of gift. The competition for the Cup was revitalised and a new chapter was about to be written.

The Squadron invited Charles A. Nicholson, Arthur Robb, James McGruer, and David Boyd each to submit two sets of lines. At the Saunders-Roe tank on the Isle of Wight nine models were tested until finally design 'B' by David Boyd was selected for the 17th Challenge. On the American side good old *Vim* was brought back to life and joined by three new Twelves, especially designed for the defence. The new boats were *Easterner* by Ray Hunt, *Weatherly* by Philip Rhodes, and *Columbia* by Olin Stephens. Convinced that any successful new boat could only be a refinement of the 1939 *Vim*, Henry Sears had asked Olin Stephens, the sole possessor of *Vim*'s lines and tank data, to work on a new design for the defence. Olin drew his variations on a winning theme and ran six models down the Hoboken tank comparing the results

TOP LEFT: Columbia *under spinnaker at Needles in 2001.*
BELOW: Columbia *raced and cruised the Mediterranean in the early Nineties until she was shipped back to the USA for a major refit at New England Boat Works.*
OPPOSITE: *A magic moment for* Columbia *and her crew.*

against the known quantities of *Vim*. *Columbia* would have slightly shorter ends and, assuming the newly developed synthetic sail fabrics would give a better drive, Olin opted for a longer waterline and a modest reduction in sail area. Comparative testing in the tank measures the progress of a yacht's design, but the acid test of performance will always remain at sea, where wind and waves create an ever-changing borderline between aero- and hydrodynamics resulting in an infinitive number of variables.

Columbia was skippered by Briggs Cunningham, an experienced yachtsman who successfully raced 6- and 12-Metres, most notably as team member on board *Vim* during her victorious season in England. The crew was made up of other great sailors such as Halsey Herreshoff, Colin Ratsey (of the sailmaking firm), Vic Romagna, Corny Shields and Rod and Olin Stephens. *Weatherly* and *Easterner* posed little threat to *Columbia*. But *Vim* did, making Olin question what he had learned since. For the answer we have to go on board *Vim*. Her skipper, Buss Mosbacher, understood match racing better than anyone and would engage *Vim* in the battle for controlling position well before the start. Briggs Cunningham on *Columbia* did not have an answer to his tactics. *Columbia* was the better boat, but the advantage was seldom enough if *Vim* had been able to win the controlling position at the start. *Columbia*'s cards changed when Cornelius Shields joined as starting helmsman. Finally *Columbia* secured her position as defender for the Cup.

Meanwhile Boyd's *Sceptre* had arrived in Newport. Her profile looked somewhat like *Vim*, but she was much fuller at the bow. When Olin first looked at *Sceptre* the memory of *Vim*

was still fresh. When asked his opinion of the challenger from Britain, all he said was, 'One of us has to be wrong'. Once the two boats met on the water the answer came loud and clear; *Columbia* was far superior under all conditions and defeated *Sceptre* 4–0 with embarrassing margins.

For the 1964 America's Cup *Columbia* entered the trials. She was defeated by *Weatherly*, sailed by Buss Mosbacher. In 1966 she was redesigned and altered by S&S. She was shortened and a bustle (a bulge in the after end of the hull, below the waterline that helps to reduce drag) was added. She stood up well against *Intrepid* but never seriously threatened her supremacy. From then on she moved to Sweden, serving as a trial horse for Pelle Peterson's *Sverige*. Her next assignment was in England, tuning up Ian Howlet's *Lionheart*. Eventually she retired to the Mediterranean but not for long: Alain Hanover shipped *Columbia* back to America and brought her back to life as a Twelve. At New England Boat Works in Portsmouth, Rhode Island, she was completely restored with a new keel by David Pedrick. As beautiful as ever, she is sailed actively from her mooring in Newport.

OPPOSITE TOP: Columbia *campaigning at La Nioulargue, St. Tropez in 1995.*
BOTTOM: *In 2001* Columbia *was shipped once more to Europe, this time to compete at the America's Cup Jubilee in Cowes.*
BELOW: Columbia *in the Solent 2001.*
FOLLOWING DOUBLE PAGE: Vim *passed the torch to* Columbia *in 1957, but not without first giving her younger sister a very hard time. Here is* Columbia *in the Solent, where* Vim *was made immortal before the War.*

Intrepid

Year of build	1967
S&S Design number	1834
Builder	Minneford Yacht Yard, City Island, New York
First owner	Intrepid Syndicate
Length overall	19.66 m
Length waterline	14.27 m
Beam	3.68 m
Draft	2.78 m
Displacement	28,348 kg

U ntil *Intrepid*, each successful new 12-Metre seemed the result of an attempt to refine the previous America's Cup winner. Few, if anyone, would have expected a breakthrough in design so outstanding as *Intrepid*, whose profile differed profoundly from the traditional fleet of Twelves. William Strawbridge, head of the 1967 syndicate, gave S&S the opportunity for an exhaustive research programme. In total seven models were built and some 55 variations ran down the tank before the final shape of *Intrepid* was drawn up. The new design sported some radical features: the long keel which had become the custom was cut back and the rudder was separated, leaving a small trim tab attached to the keel. Tests had shown the trim tab reduced leeway without increasing resistance and so improved the performance to windward. The helmsman now had three wheels to control, one for the rudder, one for the trim tab, and one to lock the two, the latter giving the boat an extraordinary turning ability. The list of innovations went on as every item on the boat was meticulously evaluated.

Her mast was of aluminium alloy with a titanium top, the coffee grinders were placed below deck to lower the centre of gravity of both crew and hardware. This, in turn, led to the idea of

TOP: *Every 12-Metre has them on board: fearless acrobats ready to climb the mast to do whatever has to be done under any condition.*
BELOW: Intrepid *sliding downwind off Cowes.*
OPPOSITE: Intrepid *is one of Olin's very best Twelves. Here she's seen from a helicopter hovering over the Jubilee course in 2001.*

bringing the boom much closer to the deck, improving the aspect ratio of the mainsail as well as reducing the induced drag. Her knuckled bow and short stern are all signs of weight reduction and the final result was a 12-Metre that would outclass all afloat and remain a benchmark for Metre-boat design for years to come.

The battle against weight revealed her Achilles heel for the defence – she twice lost her mast. One day, while Olin Stephens inspected a broken spreader fitting which had contributed to *Intrepid*'s lost mast, the wife of one of the crew members came up to him and quite innocently remarked, 'Looks very light to me.' Olin's response was, 'Well, under any other circumstances I would consider that a compliment.' In search of the material's strength boundaries, the crew showed little mercy to *Intrepid*. When later asked to reflect on the events of 1967 Olin said: 'I felt the importance of saving weight, still the *Intrepid* crew were able to remove a few pounds that the builder had used and the designer had overlooked.'

Having the outstanding yachtsman Buss Mosbacher as her skipper certainly contributed to *Intrepid*'s early success. With more 12-Metre miles than any other sailor, Mosbacher was one of the world's most experienced yachtsmen and Metre-boat sailors of his time. In 1958, against the new S&S *Columbia*, he drove good old *Vim* impossibly close to defending the Cup and in 1964 he successfully defended the Cup with *Weatherly*. He would sail every race as if his life depended on it and his complete dedication rubbed off on his crew. Racing a Twelve is not a job for an average sailor, and a sophisticated racing machine like *Intrepid* requires an expert. Buss Mosbacher and his crew had it all. *Constellation* and

a modified S&S *Columbia* merely presented a slight threat in light air downwind. *Intrepid* convincingly won the trials and continued to take the honours over *Dame Pattie*, the Australian challenger. By ordinary standards *Dame Pattie* was a good boat, but *Intrepid* was no ordinary boat and won the defence with embarrassing margins.

For the 1970 defence two new Twelves were built, *Valiant* to an S&S design and *Heritage* by Charles Morgan. Both boats were the product of extensive research and test programmes but the promises from the tank misled the architects with a disappointing result. Neither boat proved a match for *Intrepid*, which had been altered by Britton Chance. Whether these modifications made her a faster boat remains questionable but she certainly had enough to be selected as the next defender. With a 4–1 score skipper Bill Ficker drove *Intrepid* to victory over the Australian Challenger *Gretel II*. Again American supremacy in yachting was clear and the America's Cup remained safe and sound in the NYYC.

In the Nineties *Intrepid* underwent a major refit and today she is actively sailed from her home in Newport, Rhode Island. She will always remain a hallmark of innovation and brilliance from the office of Sparkman & Stephens and she sits firmly in the row of Olin's very best designs.

ABOVE: *Relaxed concentration on board* Intrepid.
OPPOSITE: Intrepid *forging to windward*.
FOLLOWING DOUBLE PAGE: *Ease the sheets, we are going home:* Intrepid *on her way in to the Royal Yacht Squadron in Cowes.*

Courageous

Year of build	1974
S&S Design number	2085
Builder	Minneford Yacht Yard, City Island, New York
First owner	Courageous Syndicate
Length overall	19.94 m
Length waterline	13.71 m
Beam	3.73 m
Draft	2.64 m
Displacement	25,000 kg

Courageous is one of those legendary S&S yachts that will always have a certain charismatic excitement about her. Having twice successfully defended the America's Cup, she was Olin's best 12-Metre of the Seventies. S&S, as well as other designers, had long recognised the advantage of aluminium as an excellent material for boatbuilding. It was, however, not until 1971, when the new scantling rules for the Twelves were introduced, that its use was permitted for the America's Cup. *Courageous* was the first Twelve by S&S after this change of rule and the choice of material was an easy one. Compared to the wooden *Intrepid*, *Courageous*'s light aluminium hull saved more than a ton, of which a good proportion would move down the keel, handsomely increasing her stability and upwind performance. The trials of 1974 soon showed her potential but, as expected, her older S&S stable-mates would give plenty of stiff competition and *Intrepid* was still the boat to beat. *Courageous*'s record improved when a young sailor named Dennis Conner joined the crew. Conner soon proved himself a talented and aggressive starting helmsman but still Ted Hood on *Intrepid* was able to sail past *Courageous* on a close spinnaker reach. The real difference came when Hood swapped boats and took the wheel of the new S&S Twelve; *Courageous* was in for the defence against *Southern Cross*, the challenger from Australia.

TOP: *Number One, the man out on the front end. Preparing for the start, his eyes are the eyes of the helmsman, who won't move up or down without a signal.*
BELOW: Courageous *under spinnaker.*
OPPOSITE: Courageous *simply has no slow mode. Here she smashes her way to windward during the 1986 World Championships off Freemantle, Australia.*

Losing the challenge 4–0, *Southern Cross* turned out to be a disappointment for her designer Ben Lexcen; the Cup was to remain bolted down in the trophy room of the NYYC. But the 1974 America's Cup was just the beginning of a 10-year quest for Ben Lexcen that would ultimately result in the removal of the Holy Grail from her pedestal. For Dennis Conner it was the start of a life's commitment to the America's Cup. As for *Courageous*, her fame developed to mythical proportions during her second defence in the 1977 competition.

Ted Turner, also known as 'Captain Outrageous', secured *Courageous* for the 1977 defence selection. Despite the knowledge that new boats would be built, Turner firmly believed in *Courageous* and, most of all, in himself. *Courageous* had a beautiful motion at sea and was certainly the best 12-Metre on the water. Turner was a talented sailor with a dedicated crew, and Turner was loud, very loud, with no appreciation for authority. With Ted's determination, hard work and talent he managed to work *Courageous* up to a consistent top performer. So much so, that before the selection committee of the NYYC had decided on the defender, he sailed up to the Australians and led his crew singing 'Waltzing Mathilda' on the aft deck. In between races Ted decided it was time to get away from it all and entered his S&S Offshore Racer *Tenacious* for the 270-mile Vineyard Race. With a last-minute crew made up from *Courageous* and *Independence*, Turner motored up to the start and quickly assigned the jobs to the crew. 'Mass confusion,' Turner hailed to a competitor alongside. 'I don't know how we will do. We're all used to sailing just 24 miles round the cans, after that we'll

probably fall asleep.' Ted didn't leave the wheel and *Tenacious* won the race.

Ted Turner had just started his Cable News Network (CNN) and, with his flamboyant personality, singlehandedly takes the credit for transforming the America's Cup into a media event. The cameras and the public loved him. Sometimes the sailing seemed no more than an interlude between his press conferences. On the water, the defence against Alan Bond's *Australia* was hardly exciting; Turner knew his *Courageous* had the speed and he convincingly led the Australians home. After he won his first race against them he said, 'Last time on *Mariner* we lost by 10 minutes, but this summer has been great, we were always close enough to hear the gun, even when we lost.' Turner continued his defence for the Cup and secured it in style with a 4–0 victory, making both himself and *Courageous* immortal.

Courageous continued her career and remained a boat to beat during selections for the America's Cup in 1980 and 1983 when she was so beautifully sailed by John Kolius. She even made it to Fremantle for her fifth attempt in 1987. Whether it was her undying S&S performance or that extraordinary feeling surrounding her, no one ever dared to lay-up the great boat named *Courageous*.

ABOVE: Courageous *looking for a favourable starting position.*
OPPOSITE TOP: *Genoa down, the Stars & Stripes up.* Courageous *on her way home.*
FOLLOWING DOUBLE PAGE: Courageous *entered her fifth America's Cup competition in 1987. She didn't make it to the finals but she sure gave some stiff competition.*

Freedom

Year of build	1979
S&S Design number	2368
Builder	Minneford Yacht Yard, City Island, New York
First owner	The Maritime College of the Fort Schuyler Foundation Inc.
Length overall	18.97 m
Length waterline	13.76 m
Beam	3.73 m
Draft	2.74 m
Displacement	26,367 kg

Although by 1979 Olin Stephens had retired from active designing, his unquestioned commitment to defending the America's Cup resulted in his returning to the office when S&S was asked to design a new 12-Metre for the 1980 defence. Olin worked closely with Bill Langan who was now chief designer at S&S. Since 1937 Olin had supplied all but one Cup defender and his dominance in 12-Metre design had not been seriously challenged for decades. *Courageous* had twice defended the Cup with only minor modifications which strengthened the widely held belief that the 12-Metre Rule left little room for further development. In a poor economic climate there was little funding available for research and design. *Courageous* was the benchmark and with the limited research budget it was not likely that *Freedom* would take a great departure from the previously proven concept.

The test model previously used for *Courageous* was to run down the tank again with small changes to the keel. Judgement supported by calculation led to a slightly lower freeboard, increasing stability while taking a small penalty on sail area; the overall layout had less windage. Her keel was slightly shorter, improving the turning abilities and suiting the aggressive sailing style of Dennis Conner.

TOP: Freedom *won her class in the 2001 America's Cup Jubilee.*
MIDDLE AND LEFT: *Dennis Conner sailed* Freedom *in 1984 during the 12-Metre Championships off Porto Cervo, Sardinia.*
OPPOSITE: Freedom US-40 *at the Costa Esmeralda, seen from the sky.*

In her trials she was up against *Courageous* and *Clipper*, a design by David Pedrick. Tuning up with *Enterprise*, *Freedom* had been in the water for over a year; Conner's preparations were intense and included shipping his boats to California for the winter. Once back in Newport he sailed *Freedom* convincingly and dominated the trials. She proved to be the better boat, outperforming *Courageous*. *Clipper* was certainly a good boat but suffered from an inexperienced crew. The choice for the selection committee was not a difficult one and *Freedom* was in for the defence.

The America's Cup finals against the Ben Lexcen design, *Australia*, may have been a sign of things to come. Although *Freedom* held the Cup with a 4–1 victory over *Australia*, the winning margin was smaller than ever. In two races the gap was

less than a minute and one race was won by the men from 'down under'. Although still not enough to win the Cup, Australian 12-Metre design had obviously advanced. Recognising this, the 1980 Cup finals stimulated the Australians, who once again stepped up their research efforts to a level that could only be compared to the *Intrepid* project. Much to Olin's regret the reverse could be said for the American side. Funding that in the past had been available for design research was now diverted to exhaustive multiple-boat campaigns with emphasis on crew and sail development. The 1983 match would prove who was right and who was wrong.

Freedom continued to be the boat to beat but an unfortunate modification by Johan Valentijn invalidated her rating certificate. This limited the choice of boats and, ultimately, *Liberty*

was chosen to defend the Cup in 1983. The Australians reaped the reward of their tireless research effort with *Australia II*, a star Twelve with a revolutionary wing-keel design. The Valentijn-designed *Liberty* was no match for the Australians who sailed to victory with a 3–4 score. The superb sailing and boat handling of Conner and his crew merely saved the Americans the embarrassment of losing the America's Cup 0–4. The final result was the same; after 132 years, the longest winning streak in the history of sport was broken.

After 1983 *Freedom*'s career would continue as a trial horse for the Italian America's Cup challenge. The French Challenge then used her to tune up their *French Kiss* for the 1987 campaign, after which she was retired from active racing. In the year 2000 she was bought by Ernest Jacquet who shipped her over to the yard of New England Boats in Portsmouth, Rhode Island. There the cruising interior was removed and *Freedom* was brought back to what Olin had in mind when she first left the drawing board. Today *Freedom* is kept in top shape and actively sailed from her new home in Newport, Rhode Island. She was the last 12-Metre to successfully defend the America's Cup for the NYYC and, judging by performance, she was the best Sparkman & Stephens 12-Metre ever.

ABOVE: Freedom *roaring along with eased sheets in a fresh breeze.*
FOLLOWING DOUBLE PAGE: *Dennis Conner at the wheel of the boat he sailed to vicory in the 1980 America's Cup.*

157

Index

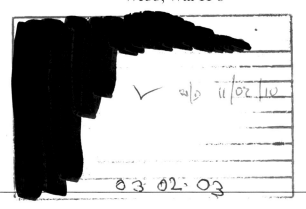